Unkind
Words

UNKIND WORDS

Ethnic Labeling from
Redskin to *WASP*

IRVING LEWIS ALLEN

BERGIN & GARVEY
New York · Westport, Connecticut · London

Library of Congress Cataloging-in-Publication Data

Allen, Irving Lewis.
    Unkind words : ethnic labeling from *Redskin* to *WASP* / Irving Lewis
Allen.
        p. cm.
    Includes bibliographical references.
    ISBN 0-89789-217-8 (alk. paper).—ISBN 0-89789-220-8 (pbk. :
alk. paper)
    1. English language—Social aspects—United States. 2. English
language—United States—Slang. 3. United States—Ethnic relations.
4. Stereotype (Psychology). 5. Ethnic groups—Slang.
6. Americanisms. 7. Epithets. I. Title.
PE2846.A46   1990
306.4'4'0973—dc20   90-32392

Library of Congress Catalog Card Number: 90-32392
ISBN: 0-89789-217-8
ISBN: 0-89789-220-8 (pbk.)

First published in 1990

Bergin & Garvey, One Madison Avenue, New York, NY 10010
An imprint of Greenwood Publishing Group, Inc.

Printed in the United States of America

The paper used in this book complies with the
Permanent Paper Standard issued by the National
Information Standards Organization (Z39.48-1984).

10 9 8 7 6 5 4 3 2 1

CONTENTS

PREFACE

American slang is among the most elaborate, fanciful, and colorful in the world, reflecting the social diversity, rapid change, and complexity of American society. Perhaps the most frequently occurring topic in historical American slang is ethnic slurs. Well over a thousand abusive nicknames aimed at more than one hundred different American ethnic groups have been recorded in dictionaries and other studies of our popular speech. Nearly every ethnic group—majority and minority alike—has slurred nearly every other group in the country. The profusion of these words speaks to one of the most troublesome aspects of our national social history. Yet the terms of abuse themselves can yield a special insight into the social workings of American society and culture, both past and present.

Beginning in the late 1960s and early 1970s, Americans have seen an upsurge of popular interest in ethnic origins, ethnic identity, and the workings of the plural society. People of all ethnic groups rediscovered their ethnicities and those of others. Scholars of American society, especially historians and social scientists, began to dredge up the dark side of our national past to help understand why we are the way we are. The history of our popular speech has proved to be an unexpectedly rich source of information about our collective self and our cultural foibles.

The slang of ethnic abuse, as offensive as it usually is, nonetheless displays the past and present tenor of ethnic relations in this country and tells an eminently American story. I will look at the major traditional themes in making ethnic slurs and at the most recent fads of covert and devious slurring with codewords and various kinds of sly word games. The language of ethnic conflict certainly has its dark side but often as not it is just low comedy.

The first half of the book deals with the older and more traditional slurs in American vernaculars. The most offensive words among these are the old "fighting words" that—when dropped—raised fists in schoolyards and barrooms. Most of these words have had their day, and even the best known among them are today rarely heard in earnest public discourse. The old fighting words are displayed here in a "word museum" where we can see some of the viciousness and foolishness of our cultural past.

The second half deals with another order of ethnic labeling. These terms, many of them new words that have appeared in the past few decades, are often more genteel and less confrontational. While less direct, they sometimes still serve the same old psychological and social needs to stereotype and express hostility. George Orwell, in his famous essay of 1946, "Politics and the English Language," wrote: "But if thought corrupts language, language can also corrupt thought. A bad usage can spread by tradition and imitation, even among people who should and do know better."

Among the newer words are a number of euphemisms and codewords for ethnic persons and groups, some of which are well intended as "kind" words. Some of them nonetheless harbor troublesome notions of ethnic cultural differences and the relation of these supposed traits to social problems. These near-slurs are in several ways more instructive, for they show how ethnic epithets, supported by contemporary and more guarded prejudices, sometimes slip acceptably into the usages of everyday speech—and some even gain respectability in print. These words represent a new generation of ethnic slurs that are replacing the older, more blatant and abusive nicknames.

Most of the examples of these newer slurs are drawn from the writings of social critics, journalists, and social scientists who contribute to various public forums, from the national press to academic writing. The locutions of social science and the new usages that appear in public discussions of the great issues of the day greatly influence one another. Literary people, scholars, critics, and journalists often pursue common enterprises. All are scrambling to name and rename the bewildering and changing reality of ethnic and class diversity in America today. Its complexity is even harder to grasp when the thinking about it is swayed by the winds of ideology and the breezes of fad and fashion.

The message of this book is that we have too often let shoddy language shape our thinking about the politics of ethnicity. The final chapters are essays on bad usages that we have not yet completely shunned. Orwell (1946) left us with a hopeful thought. Our language

> becomes ugly and inaccurate because our thoughts are foolish, but the slovenliness of our language makes it easier for us to have foolish thoughts. The point is that the process is reversible. Modern English, especially written English, is full of bad habits which spread by imitation and which can be avoided if one is willing to take the necessary trouble. If one gets rid of these habits one can think more clearly, and to think clearly is a necessary first step towards political regeneration.

ACKNOWLEDGMENTS

Chapters 3 and 7 first appeared in the linguistics journal *Names*, December 1983 and September-December 1988; Chapter 4 in *Sex Roles*, July 1984; and Chapters 5 and 9 in *Maledicta*, 1983 and 1981, respectively. Chapter 10 draws from my article in *Ethnicity*, June 1975. All are revised and used here with the generous permissions of the publishers. Chapter 6 was first presented as a paper before the joint meetings of the American Name Society and the Modern Language Association, San Francisco, 1987.

I thank the staff, especially Robert D. Vrecenak, in the Interlibrary Loan Department of the Homer Babbidge Library at the University of Connecticut for their thoroughly professional services. They have materially aided my work.

Part I

Traditional Slurs

When you call me that, *smile*!
        —Owen Wister, in *The Virginian*, 1902

CHAPTER 1

ETHNIC SLURS IN HISTORICAL AMERICAN SLANG

ETHNIC SLURS IN historical American speech compete in number with terms for sex and related matters. Perhaps as many as twelve hundred ethnic slur-names or epithets appear in those scholarly annals and other sources that record the historical words of popular speech in our language. Most of these slurs are obsolete today, but a surprising number of the old words are still to be heard, and a few new ones seem to appear each year. Whether obsolete or current, they are of equal interest for social history.

Ethnic slurs began appearing in American English when the first British settlers came into contact with Native American Indians. *Redskin*, whose earliest known written instance is 1699, was one of the first slur-names given by white settlers to the Native Americans they encountered. The whites soon began their infamous three-hundred-year relationship with the African slaves they imported and another, larger torrent of verbal abuse was unleashed. As other groups arrived and the country became more ethnically diverse, the number of slurs grew in direct proportion. Ethnic slurs appear in response to social and economic conflict during historical periods of rapid social change. The coinage of most slurs can be associated with great events in our social history, particularly waves of immigration, urbanization, war and its aftermath, depressions, and massive migrations of labor.

This profusion of ethnic slurs in our language obviously reflects the bigotry and prejudice in our cultural history. But at a deeper level these words chronicle the history of ethnic conflict in American society. The number of slurs, their targets, and the origins of the terms show that most originated in historical situations—wherever groups met and fell into conflict. Contact and conflict, usually about economic matters, heightened the contrast of ethnic cultures, which led to culture clash and recoil. Ethnic slurs proliferated in cities where many ethnic groups lived in close quarters and bristled in their everyday contacts.

Many of the words are genuine Americanisms—homegrown words first coined and used in this country. Many others are loanwords borrowed especially from British English, but also from Spanish, French, German, Yiddish, and West African languages—the languages of major immigrant groups.

SLANG AND SLURS

Slang is difficult to define to the satisfaction of all who want to distinguish it precisely from other forms of informal speech, such as jargon, cant, and regionalisms. Linguists Bethany Dumas and Jonathan Lighter suggested a useful definition of slang: standard English nouns denote a referent, while words of slang characterize a referent and, moreover, produce a rhetorical effect. Ethnic epithets, in contrast to the proper names of groups, do exactly this. Most epithets also have those ephemeral, flippant, piquant, and outlaw qualities that make them slang.

The vocabulary of general slang is fraught with words that reach for meanings beyond the locutions of standard language, which often fails emotional needs for some subjects.

The number of slang words for various social objects indicates levels of cultural anxiety about taboo, embarrassing, and stressful subjects. A reading of Wentworth and Flexner's *Dictionary of American Slang* (1975), still the most authoritative compilation of historical slang, will show that our slang is permeated with words for ethnicity, sexuality, drunkenness, eating, excretion, violence, failure, and cheating.

Ethnic slurs, like slang in general, have been chiefly a male vocabulary of anxiety. Historically viewed, much slang is clearly an effort to deal with and to control a male social reality. Carl Sandburg said that "slang is a language that rolls up its sleeves, spits on its hands and goes to work." Ethnic slurs extend slang to "dirty work" as well. Slurs have been part of the rough language of field, factory, marketplace, and wherever diverse ethnic groups met and competed for social status, income, and jobs. These words express the anxieties, jealousies, envies, resentments, and anger of groups in conflict.

Women have used slang in general, and ethnic slurs in particular, less often than men. I venture that women's use of ethnic epithets and other slang reflects in some part commiseration and identification with male anxieties in the marketplace and has increased in this century with the greater involvement of women in the labor force outside the home.

WHAT IS AN ETHNIC GROUP?

A popular but incomplete definition of an ethnic slur is a term of abuse that members of the native-born white majority apply to members of a racial or immigrant minority. This error stems in part from the euphemistic use of *ethnic group* for only low-income, oppressed, or recently arrived immigrant groups. Many people are not yet accustomed to thinking of ethnic majorities as just other ethnic groups.

Actually, the white Protestant majority in the United States is not a single ethnic group but several. When individual white Protestants do not identify with a particular national origin, which surprisingly many do, they are often members of culturally distinct groups cut along regional, class, and denominational lines. White Southerners are the largest, most clearly defined of such groups, but there are others.

An ethnic group can be succinctly defined as any racial, religious, mother-tongue, national-origin, or regional category of culturally distinct persons, regardless of the group's size (minority or majority), social power (subordinate or dominant), or when its members immigrated to this country (immigrant, native-born, or indigenous). The *Harvard Encyclopedia of American Ethnic Groups* identifies 106 such ethnic groups who have lived in the United States. Slurs have been directed against most of these groups.

A BAD WORD FOR EVERYBODY

Ethnic slurs are not just terms of abuse that majorities have used against minorities. Some members of every ethnic group have used slurs for almost every group with whom they have had contact and economic or cultural conflict. Majorities probably have been the greater users of ethnic slurs because they had the greater interest in keeping other groups down. Yet minorities have invented and used slurs for other minorities and also plentifully for majorities. Slurs are aimed most frequently at blacks, Jews, the Irish, Italians, Mexicans, Chinese, and—it will surprise some—white Protestant groups. All these groups are among the largest or most visible groups in American society.

Ethnic groups have been berated with a variety of different slurs for the most part in direct proportion to their historical population size and to their contacts with other groups. The largest majority and the largest minority groups have had the greatest number of contact points with other groups, and the resultant conflict has spawned a commensurate number of different slurs for them. Nonetheless, racism, anti-Semitism, anti-Catholicism, and other standing cultural biases have aggravated conflict at points of intergroup contact and have increased slurs for racial and religious minorities.

Any distraction from the idea that the roots of prejudice do not all lie in the minds and hearts of the prejudiced is forever open to the charge of "blaming the victim." But social scientists have learned that situations of conflict, especially inequality, between groups produce prejudice. And the amelioration of prejudice will largely be in the relief of the most unnecessary and ruinous inequality and conflict in society.

THE SOCIAL USES OF ETHNIC SLURS

Because ethnic slurs are part of a vital language, they change over time in their connotations and in the social contexts in which they are acceptably used or not. Slurs also vary greatly in pejoration, ranging from the malicious and vicious to the puerile and jocular. The meaning of words is not inherent in the words themselves but in what the words mean to the speaker and the hearer. All ethnic slurs are offensive to some degree to some people, and this depends on the speaker, the hearer, their relationship, and the social context in which the words are used. Certain ethnic slurs may be used jocularly, even affectionately within a group. But the same word could be highly offensive if used by an outsider. A few infamous slurs have gone through a linguistic process called "inversion" and have been given positive, warmly humorous meanings within the group that was the original target of the slur. Among some African-Americans, this happened with the hated word *nigger*.

Nonetheless, the use of ethnic slurs is rightly regarded as

a social problem. Slurs reflect stereotypes that often have harmful social and psychological consequences for their victims. If the targets of ethnic slurs are secure enough in their social position, such as many members of majority groups, or just secure in their own identity, such as sophisticated members of minority groups, they can often slough off the name-calling, even laugh at the desperate tactics of the name-callers. But many individuals and groups are vulnerable, and stereotypes often have real negative consequences for the victims.

The overt purpose of an ethnic epithet is to insult and to injure. The use of ethnic slurs is also an effort, whether quite consciously realized or not, to control the behavior of the disparaged group. A primitive belief lingers in all societies that if one can name or attach a label to an object, in this case an ethnic individual or group, then one can wield power over it simply by calling its name.

Most ethnic epithets amount to nicknames for ethnic persons or groups. If the name is abusive, denigrating, scolding, or ridiculing, it is expected that calling the name will cause the victim to cower, to be denigrated, to be scolded and thus to feel guilty, or to act out the prophecy of the stereotype. Usually this prophecy is fulfilled in the eye of the beholder by their seeing only what they expect and want to see in the real behavior of the group over which they seek control.

For the victims, the social psychology of being controlled is to acquire a false self-image. Minority group members, like everyone else, accept many if not most values of the society they live in, including sometimes the stereotypical images of themselves. Blacks, for example, in the past had many nicknames for other African Americans that were a system of color-caste coding and signaled an acceptance of one criterion of white racism. The eventual self-derogation of a group is one of the most tragic implications of the use of ethnic slurs. Groups have sometimes not only accepted the stereotyped image of themselves but unwittingly played into the hands of the prejudiced by acting out the prophecy. They have then affirmed the stereotyped image of the prejudiced—and they are controlled.

Yet minorities, particularly blacks, have resisted stereotypes in creative ways. Folklorist Roger D. Abrahams in his book *Positively Black* (1970) tells how broader stereotypes, such as thievery, sexual abandon, childishness, and laziness, through a social psychological process called "conversion," are acted out as techniques of aggression and ridicule against whites.

All this brings us to the deeper social meaning of the profusion of ethnic slurs in American English. Words are weapons, and "hurling" epithets is a universal trait of hostile intergroup relations. Ethnic slurs are preeminently a political vocabulary. Name-calling is a technique by which outgroups—"them" as opposed to "us"—are defined as morally-just targets of aggression. It is an effort to control other groups by neutralizing their efforts to gain social and economic power or to influence the values of society. For majorities, the use of ethnic slurs justifies inequality and discrimination by giving a perverse logic to invidious comparisons of ethnic differences. In short, ethnic slurs are used to produce and maintain social class and privilege. For minorities, name-calling often redresses the injuries of class and the social injustice of privilege and tries to dignify an imposed minority status.

ETHNIC SLURS AS URBAN FOLKLORE

Folklorists such as Alan Dundes and Roger D. Abrahams regard ethnic slurs as part of the folklore of modern, urban society. Ethnic slurs are usefully viewed as part of the lore of ethnic groups in conflict, each seeking to maintain its own status and identity, especially in the close quarters of big-city life. Many ethnic slurs and their associated meanings are, in effect, the self-expression of a group's relations with other groups.

The folkloric use of ethnic slurs can be illustrated with the popular but false stories about how certain terms of abuse supposedly originated. The epithets *wop*, *guinea*, *canuck*, *kike*, *ofay*, and *honky* are each richly embellished with several spurious stories of their origins. These little narratives are best understood as parables or allegories. Specious etymologies are often symbolic narratives with ritual situations of conflict, heroes, villains, and a moral point concerning ethnic relations. For those who use a slur, these stories or folktales seem to justify the term. Other stories are favored by the victims to dignify the derogation of the term.

To take just one example, *wop*, the derogatory and offensive nickname for an Italian American, derives from the Neapolitan and Sicilian dialect's *guappo*, a strong and handsome man. *Guappo* was probably used as a greeting and a compliment among early Italian immigrants. Even today Neapolitans call themselves *guapi*—the pretty ones. Perhaps the slang term *dude* carries the nearest equivalent sense in American English. (The etymology of *dude* is uncertain, but it dates back to the 1880s and is thought to refer to clothes— *duds*.) By the mid-1890s, near the peak of Italian immigration, *wop* appeared in American slang as a derogatory epithet for Italian men. In some way, *guappo* was borrowed by name-callers and the last syllable dropped.

A popular but probably wrong story has it that *wop* is an acronym for the phrase *W*ith-*O*ut *P*apers (or *P*assport) or sometimes *W*ithout *O*fficial *P*apers. Alan Dundes, writing in the *Journal of American Folklore* (1971), relates one version, "that in the early 1920s many Italians tried to enter the United States illegally. These would-be immigrants were rounded up by U. S. officials and sent back to Italy with documents labelled W. O. P., which supposedly stood for 'Without Papers' referring to the papers needed for legal immigration." This story, if it is entirely untrue, has the makings of folklore. As the story is variously embellished, the hopeful immigrants are pitted against the indifference of immigration officials and the crass bureaucracy of Ellis Island and labelled *wops*, as though they were less than human. History does tell us that many immigrants were processed meanly and roughly. This story, which is symbolic of the immigration experience, is an obvious allegory for the attitudes of old immigrants toward new immigrants.

Because ethnic slurs are part of our folklore, many entered the mainstream of our popular culture and were transmitted by the mass media, sanctioning them for the millions. As the country became more industrialized in the nineteenth century and the cities more diverse, the mass media, beginning with minstrelsy and vaudeville, reflected more and more the concerns, the interests, and the social worlds of their mainly urban audiences. The mass media have had a special role in creating a vitality and popularity of ethnic slurs. The use of ethnic slurs in everyday speech has been long reinforced by, and reflected in, the public media of print, popular songs, radio, movies, and most recently television. Examples are legion.

H. L. Mencken related the famous story of how the slur *coon* for African Americans was introduced in vaudeville and later popularized by a hit song of 1896, "All Coons Look Alike to Me," by Ernest Hogan, a black man, who did not intend it as a slur. Hogan probably thought that *coon* was just a conventional, humorous nickname for his group in show business and he accepted it; people were not so slur conscious in those days. Yet when Hogan later understood the adverse reaction of his people to the song, he was crushed with remorse. Don B. Wilmeth in *The Language of American Popular Entertainment* (1981) relates how the so-called coon songs performed in minstrel shows around the turn of the century purveyed vicious stereotypes of blacks.

As much as some would hope, ethnic slurs are not just a

historical curiosity in the American language. Popular culture and serious works of literature throughout our history
have kept ethnic slurs before our eyes and in our minds.
The movies, ever since they began talking, sprinkled their
dialogues with period slurs, often in earnest in the 1930s
and 1940s, though more self-consciously after the Second
World War and to the present day. In the 1970s, television's "Archie Bunker" in his first incarnation did much to
take the old slur *jungle bunny* and others off city streets and
into suburban living rooms. Novelists have long used ethnic
slurs to create literary realism. Big-city color writers, such
as Theodore Dreiser, John Dos Passos, James T. Farrell, John
O'Hara, Damon Runyon, Nelson Algren, Raymond Chandler and, lately, John Sayles and John Gregory Dunne have
used period epithets to lace the dialogue of their characters.

At the same time, public sensitivity to ethnic slurs has
never been higher, and now and then politicians and other
public figures perversely oblige their critics with an ill-con-
sidered word. Many in the nation were shocked at President
Nixon's talk of "Jew boys" on the infamous tapes. Earl Butts,
the former Secretary of Agriculture, committed political
suicide in front of reporters with his racist jokes about blacks.
Spiro Agnew made cracks about "Polacks." The obvious political liability of letting a slur slip out inspired the 1970
Nixon campaign of "dirty tricks," where they planted a rumor that Democratic candidate Edmund Muskie has spoken
of "Canucks" in Maine, which he had not. In 1984, Presidential candidate Jesse Jackson damaged his cause with a
careless remark to a *Washington Post* reporter about "Hymie"—his Jewish critics—and "Hymietown"—New York
City.

Ethnic slurs are alive and well in American life, though
usually in more muted and devious forms. In later chapters
I will try to root out the newest slurs that, like some of the

old slurs, masquerade as objective language—just calling a spade a spade. But first let us look at the variety of ways slurs have occurred in language and at the kinds of allusions they have made to do their dirty work.

CHAPTER 2

SIX TYPES OF SLURS AND THEIR THEMES

ETHNIC SLURS TRADITIONALLY occur in language and culture in a variety of forms, such as derisive nicknames for groups, several kinds of metaphors, children's rhymes and sayings, and the famous ethnic jokes. The epithet or nickname is the most frequent form, though the other kinds of slurs are plentiful in our cultural history. I will describe each type of slur with a few examples before turning to the most common type and the subject of this book—the derogatory name.

Scholars of American folklore have recorded scores of derisive adjectives taken from the proper names of ethnic groups. This particular device is most often used to slur the Mexicans, the Irish, the Jews, the blacks, the Dutch, the Chinese, and the French. Examples are *Mexican breakfast* for a cigarette and a glass of water, *Irish spoon* for a shovel, *Jew flag* for a dollar bill, *Chinese B* for an unearned grade in college, *Dutch courage* for the foolhardiness that comes with drink, *French leave* for being absent without leave from the military, and *African golf* for the dice game of craps. Such terms are still used now and then. Columnist William Safire (January 17, 1983), for example, referred to organizational problems in the White House as a *Chinese firedrill*, a term for any situation in disarray.

The proper names of groups have also been converted to derisive verb forms, which are familiar to speakers of English. *To dutch* is to ruin with malice; *to french* is to fellate; *to nigger* is to ruin with carelessness; *to out-yankee* is to outsmart; *to welsh* is to renege; *to gyp* is to cheat; *to jew* is to cheat or *to jew down* is to bargain ruthlessly; *to jap* is to attack without warning; and *to scotch* is to squelch.

Ethnic slurs also appear in a form that the linguist John Algeo calls "ethnicons," a kind of metaphor, such as *swede* for a blunderer, *turk* for a cruel, aggressive person, or for a sodomite, *arab* for a footloose person or a peddler, *scotchman* for a miserly person, *welsher* for a reneger, *pole* for a dumb person, *indian* for a reckless or wild person, or *mormon* for a lecher, *tartar* for an intractable person, *hessian* for a mercenary, *yankee* for a swindler or a shrewd bargainer, *greek* for a cheat at cards, and others.

Sayings in folklore often amount to ethnic slurs. A. A. Roback, who was one of the first social scientists to collect and study ethnic slurs, records many of these proverbs, and many are American in origin. Some are sayings, such as "A Scotchman is one who keeps the Sabbath and every other thing he can lay his hands on." Others are similes, such as "Resolute as a drunken Irishman." Traditional children's rhymes have long had taunting ethnic slurs. The most familiar one is surely: "Eeney-meeney-miney-moe! / Catch a nigger by the toe! / If he hollers, let him go! / Eeney-meeney-miney-moe!" The racial and ethnic taunts of children can be vicious and damaging to the victims. The late Peter Opie (1970), the folklorist of children's lore, wrote that the well-known doggerel on name-calling should be rephrased: "Sticks and stones just break my bones. / It's words that really hurt me."

The joke is one of the most prevalent forms of folklore in modern society, and the ethnic joke is one of the most popular types, especially the ethnic "numbskull" jokes and riddles. The riddles tend to cluster about certain situations: How many Poles (or Italians, Germans, WASPs, Jewish mothers, etc.) does it take to change a light bulb? In the past, numbskull jokes and riddles have been vicious, but folklorist Roger D. Abrahams recently wrote in the *Harvard Encyclopedia of American Ethnic Groups* (1980) that the enormous popularity of these jokes and riddles signals not so much prejudice and bigotry but a certain good-natured, mirthful acceptance of cultural pluralism. At least, the profusion of these jokes in print and in polite company these days is not meeting with the indignant objections that one might expect considering the coarse stereotypes they represent. Nonetheless, Polish groups still protest.

Undoubtedly, the most numerous and varied type of ethnic slur is the epithet or generic nickname for ethnic persons and groups. More than fifty different American ethnic groups have been dubbed with one or scores of epithets; well over a thousand of these have been recorded in the history of American English.[1] Many of these terms certainly were never widely used in the general language but had only local and passing use. Yet most have been recorded in more than one scholarly source and all are believable.

If epithets were added for quasi-ethnic groups, such as the hundreds of terms for poor whites and rustics, mostly various white Protestant groups, the number of ethnic epithets in historical American slang and dialect would rise to nearly two thousand terms. In the remaining pages of this chapter and in the chapters that follow, I will deal with only this most numerous type of ethnic slur—the epithet or nickname for ethnic persons and groups.

Patterns of meaning in the huge aggregate of these terms can best be seen by sorting and counting the terms that fall into various thematic categories—the various supposed physical and cultural traits of groups—and by giving a representative variety of examples of each theme.

PHYSICAL TRAITS

About one in five ethnic epithets in American English refers to supposed physical traits of groups. These are allusions to color, to shapes of eyes, heads, noses, and lips, and
to hair texture. Epithets that refer to physical traits are mostly
interracial slurs. Nearly half of all interracial slurs (whites
slurring blacks, Asians, and Native Americans—and these
racial minorities slurring whites) refer to real or imagined
physical differences. Whites have called Asian-American
groups *slant eyes* and Asians have begun calling whites *round
eyes* as a comeback. Jews were called *eagle beaks* and blacks
broad noses. African Americans were also called *wooly heads*
and blacks, in turn, called whites *silks*, an allusion to thin-
ner, straighter hair.

Most references to physical differences are to skin color,
which affirms what we have always known about the signif-
icance of color in human relations. Asian groups were called
yellow this and that and Native Americans were called *red-
skins*, *red men*, and *red devils*. Most slurs on skin color appear
in the name-calling between whites and blacks. Whites have
slurred blacks with a profusion of terms that allude to dark
skin (*blue*, *darky*, *shade*, *smoke*) and blacks, tit for tat, have
slurred whites (*chalk*, *grey*, *pink*, *pale*). A large number of
white terms for African Americans were *black* this or that,
such as *black bird*, or else a word for something—anything—
black in color, such as *coal*, *charcoal*, *skillet*, *tarpot*, and a host
of others.

CHOCOLATE IS BROWN AND SO ARE YOU

A bizarre feature of making derisive names about color
differences is the many references to the color of foods. A
perennially popular derisive name for African Americans is

chocolate and its variants *chokker* and *chokko*. Johnny Carson, during his show on September 17, 1981, tastelessly joked about dipping a white baby "in chocolate and sub him in for Gary Coleman." The studio audience booed. Blacks have also been called *licorice, raisin, mocha* (probably from the dark blend of chocolate and coffee), and *molonjohn* (from Italian-American street slang, deriving from Italian *melanzana*, eggplant). Black women in particular have been given the name of sweets, such as *chocolate drop, hot chocolate, sweet chocolate, brown sugar* and its reverse *sugar brown*, and some of these terms have been used affectionately among blacks as well. Blacks have not missed this opportunity and have called whites names such as *marshmallow, milk, vanilla*, and the punning name *soda cracker*.

In the past, more than today, meats were smoked as a preservative, giving them a dark color. African Americans in the nineteenth century were derisively called *smoked Irishmen* and *smoked Yankees*. Native Americans were called *smoked ham* and *smokey*. Referring to their light brown but supposedly "yellow" color, Chinese Americans were sometimes called *mustard*. Racially mixed persons of black and white ancestry were cruelly called *mustard yellow, pumpkin yellow*, and girls and women particularly, *banana* and *lemon*.

Food items that are one color on the outside but white on the inside have become metaphors to scold social assimilators within ethnic groups. These words are ethnic slurs used within groups. The most famous is surely *oreo* from Nabisco's chocolate wafer, creme-filled Oreo cookies ("black on the outside but white on the inside"); *oreo* or *oreo cookie* was sometimes coded to just *cookie*. Native Americans were soon chastising those among them who would conciliate too much with whites with the name *apple* ("red on the outside but . . . "). The Chinese followed with *banana*.

CULTURAL DIFFERENCES AND OTHER SOCIAL SYMBOLS

Regardless of the frequency of references to supposed physical differences in making ethnic slurs, the vast majority of ethnic epithets refer to various nonphysical stereotypes of groups, such as supposed character traits, symbols of religious differences, personal names thought common in the group, dietary stereotypes, and many other real and imagined cultural differences. I will also include in this category the name-calling that is nothing more than word plays on and alterations of the proper names of groups.

This greater number of epithets in our historical slang that carp on putative social and cultural traits of groups are equally offensive but they tend to be more history laden and to reveal more of the cultural, social, and economic conflict among ethnic groups—what prejudice is ultimately about more than anything else. In the remaining pages of this chapter and in the chapters that follow, I will discuss the major cultural and social themes in making ethnic epithets.

References to supposed group or national character account for more than one in ten of all ethnic epithets in the American language. These words reflect the old stereotypes that Jews are crafty, Mexicans are lazy, Poles are dumb, Germans are authoritarian, Irishmen are drunks, Scots are miserly, and so on. These epithets allude to putative mental traits, such as personality, character, intelligence, morality, and political beliefs. Overt behavioral traits also are sometimes alluded to, such as civility, grooming, sexual appetite, and demeanor. A few examples are *lightning* for a black, *dummerhead* for a German, *asshole bandit* for a Greek, *whisky mick* for an Irishman, *mafia* for an Italian, *Shylock* for a Jew, *never sweat* for a Mexican, *dumb polack* for a Pole, *pinch penny* for a Scot, *rednecks* for certain ethnic Southerners, *dumbsocks* for a Swede, and *eel*, an old word for a Yankee in New England.

About one in eight epithets are simply alterations of the proper names of groups, such as *'jin* for a Native American, *ay-rab* for anyone from an Arab group, *orsestralian* for an Australian, *belgie* for a Belgian, *basco* for a Basque, *chink* for a Chinese, *chessie* for a Czech, *esky* for an Eskimo, *fip* or *flip* for a Filipino, *frencher* for a Frenchman, *gerry* for a German, *gyp* for a gypsy, *hunky* for a Hungarian, *irisher* for an Irishman, *eyetie* for an Italian, *jap* for an Japanese, *jewy* for a Jew, *lit* for a Lithuanian, *mexie* for a Mexican, *norsky* for a Norwegian, *paki* for a Pakistani, *portagee* for a Portuguese, *P. R.* for a Puerto Rican, *rusky* for a Russian, *scotty* for a Scot, *spinach* for a Spaniard, and *waler* for a Welshman.

About four in ten epithets refer to a large variety of other cultural themes, such as folk costumes popularly associated with a group (e. g., *kiltie* for a Scotsman). A number of terms are references to religious differences, mostly aimed at Catholics, Jews, and Protestant sects. These names allude to symbols, such as the cross (*crossback*), Mariolatry (*statue worshipper*), rosaries (*bead puller*), and the Pope (*poper*) for Catholics; circumcision (*clip dick*) and dietary law (*porker*) for Jews; and ecstatic religiosity (*Jesus screamer*, *holy roller*) for Protestant sects.

A score of epithets are various kinds of phonic mimicry that ridicule the sounds of foreign languages (*pong* for the Chinese) or make mocking allusion to stereotyped foreign-language phrases (*parleyvoo* and *dee-donk*, from the sound of *dis donc*, roughly "hey, tell me," for the French). I have found about thirty terms that refer to stereotypical occupations held in low esteem, such as menial or migrant labor (*wetback* for Mexicans), or to stigmatized occupations, such as money-lending, huckstering, and peddling (*shonky* and *smous* for Jews).[2] As many as fifty slang terms refer to low-status places of residence. Older terms of rural origin, such as *pineywoods pecker* for a poor white Southerner, deride residence on land of small economic value in an agrarian society, such as swamps (*swamp rat* for an Acadian) or brushwoods (*brush ape* for a Southern highlander). More recent terms derogate residence in low-status urban environments, such as slums (*ghetto ghoul* for a black), and cities (*jew norker* and *city boy* for Jews).

In the chapters that follow, I will take a more detailed look at yet other major cultural themes in making ethnic slurs, specifically the many personal names that became ethnic epithets, the terms of abuse that men have applied to ethnic women, particularly women of racial minorities, the profusion of dietary stereotypes in ethnic epithets, quasi-ethnic epithets for our homegrown regional and poor white groups, and the recent fad of making ethnic epithets with acronyms.

NOTES

1. My statements about the numbers of slurs in American English for various groups and, later, about the numbers of epithets with various themes are based on calculations reported in chapter 4 of my book *The Language of Ethnic Conflict* (1983).

2. Partridge, for example, suggests that *shonky* derives from Yiddish *shonnicker*, a small-time trader or peddler. Similarly, *smous* has sometimes meant a Jewish peddler, probably in the sense of a patterer.

CHAPTER 3

TWO HUNDRED PERSONAL NAMES THAT BECAME EPITHETS

MANY PERSONAL NAMES, mostly given or first names, came to be used as generic nicknames for persons of various ethnic groups over the course of American social history. I found about two hundred such terms for thirty-five different ethnic groups. About one in six of all ethnic epithets in American historical slang is formed on a personal name.

Most are names popularly associated with various groups, such as *Mike* and *Murphy* for Irishmen, *Ole* for Swedish men, *Hans* for German men, *Tony* for Italian men, *Closh* for Dutchmen, *Abe* for Jewish men, *Ivan* for Russian men, *Lize* or *Liza* for black women, and *Bridget* for Irish women. Others are personal names derived from popular historical associations, literary characters studied in the schoolroom, popular verse, folklore, and the popular culture of the mass media. A few examples are *Jeff Davis* or just *Jeff* for a white ethnic Southerner, *Hiawatha* for a Native American, *Johnny Cake* for a French Canadian, *Hans Wurst* for a German, and *Sapphire* for a black woman.

All the words in this and subsequent chapters may be found in scholarly records. Many of the terms were ephemeral, and most are now obsolete or obsolescent, though a few may be heard today. These terms were collected for the most

part from some twenty dictionaries and word lists of nine-
teenth- and twentieth-century American slang and dialect,
but also from many other scattered, diverse sources. Many
of the terms are not American coinages but are loanwords
from the languages of major immigrant groups, especially
British English. The names became Americanisms in a broad
sense when they were applied with new connotations to new
immigrants in their new American settings.

The names may be divided into three broad categories,
which sometimes overlap. First, about fifty terms are cultural symbols of anonymity and low status, such as *John* and
Charlie, which are used for a variety of different groups.
Second, over thirty names are allusions to popular historical
associations. A third and largest class is over a hundred names
that are given and family names thought common in various
ethnic groups.

JOHN AS THE SYMBOL OF ETHNIC EVERYMAN

The most frequently occurring epithet formed on a personal name is *John*, its diminutive *Johnny*, *-ie*, and through
popular usage, *Jack*, *Jock*, and *Jocko*, *John*'s feminine sound
counterparts, *Joan*, *Jane*, *Jenny*, and *John*'s foreign equivalents, *Hans*, *Ivan*, *Jean*, *Jan*, and *Sean*. Thirty epithets are
modeled on *John*, its variants and equivalents. Forms of *John*
have been applied to U. S. groups as various as blacks, Native Americans, Chinese, Japanese, Cornish, Welsh, English,
Scots, Irish, Dutch, Germans, Greeks, ethnic Southerners,
and especially the French and French Canadians. (Stuart Berg
Flexner in *Listening to America* (1982) essays on a variety of
other *John* words in American English.)

Terms of social opposition are a frequent topic in slang.
In British and American English *John* is the favored pejora-

tive denomination for outsiders—"them" as opposed to "us." For example, *John* is used for any group being held at social distance (*Johnny Chinaman*), persons being dismissed (the "Dear John" letter), anonymous or "average" persons ("John Doe"), nonpersons (the prostitute's "John"), and an easy mark or victim ("dumb John"). *John* and its equivalents are common given names in several European national cultures, which surely also influenced its use as a generic name for outsiders, especially ethnic outsiders.

Several British loanwords in American English, some borrowed earlier by the British from the French, have been used for the French in America, such as *Jean*, *Jean Crapaud* (John Toad), *Jean Potage* (John Soup), and *Johnny*. Other British loans have been extended to, and a few original Americanisms have been used for, the French Canadians: *Johnny Crapaud*, *Jean-* or *John-Baptiste*, *Jean Batiste* (that is, John Muslin), *Johnny Cake*, and *Johnny Peasoup*.

Other loans of John words from British English and their American variants have been used for British Isles groups in the United States. *Cousin Jack*, *Cousin Jacky*, *Cousin Jan*, and *Cousin Jenny* were used for the Cornish. *Cousin Jack* was also used for the Welsh. *Jock* and *Jockie* were used for Scots. *Johnny* was used for the English, as well as the old personification *John Bull* and its variant *Johnny Bull*. *Jonathan* was an early term for the Yankees of New England when most were of British descent. *Yankee* itself probably derives from *Jan Kaas*, John Cheese, which was an English epithet for the Dutch. *Jan Kaas* was somehow turned on the English of New England, where it stuck, the *-kaas* later being taken as a plural inflection.

John, *Johnny*, *John Chinaman*, and *Johnny Chinaman* were used for the Chinese. *Jocko*, a form of *Jock*, from *Jack*, was used for the Japanese. *Mister John* was used for Native American Indians. In the nineteenth century *Free Jack*, also shortened to *Jack*, was used for blacks; *Monkey Jane* is a 1920s term for a black woman. The ubiquitous *Johnny* also was used for a Greek or a Turk. *Johnny Squarehead*, *Hans*, and *Hans Wurst* were used for Germans. *Johnny Reb* was used for Southerners. *Shoneen*, the diminutive of *Seon*, that is, John, has been used for the Irish. Rural Southern blacks called poor whites *Cheap John* and *Cheap Jack*.

   Charlie is another ethnic slur resembles *John* and *Johnny* in its uses. *Charlie* otherwise has long been a pejorative name; for example, *Charlie* is the name for any clown in the slang of early show biz. *Charlie* early was used for the Chinese and recently for the Vietnamese. (*Carlo* was a rare generic name for an Italian.) But *Charlie* is today best known as a black term for whites: *Mister Charlie*, *-ey*, and *Charlie*. Wry variants are *Mister Charles*, *Charles*, and *Chuck*. For the female counterpart of *Charlie* or *Charles*, the cognate *Charlene* was briefly used.

   Other diminutive names, such as *Sammy*, *Tommy*, and *Billy* similarly have been used for outgroups. *Sammy* was used for Scots. Jews were called *Sammys*, perhaps only from *Samuel*, but Wentworth and Flexner's *Dictionary of American Slang* (1975) says that *Sammy* was influenced by the initials of Sigma Alpha Mu, a Jewish college fraternity, whose members are called *Sammys*. Ethnic Appalachian Southerners in the industrial cities of the Ohio Valley in the 1950s were called *SAMs*, an acronym for Southern Appalachian Migrants. *Tommy* was used for the English and derives from *Tommy Atkins*, the personification of British soldiers, much like G. I. Joe in the United States. (The British called American soldiers *Sammys* during the First World War, after *Uncle Sam*.) British Canadians were recently nicknamed *TOM*, an acronym, because a certain elite was thought to concentrate in Toronto, Ottawa, and Montreal, and I suspect *TOM* was also constructed to be reminiscent of *Tommy* for the English. Ethnic Appalachian Southerners have been called *Hillbillys* since about 1900; the *-billy* component is an old term for any fellow. *Hillnelly* was later modeled on *Hillbilly*.

CULTURAL ALLUSIONS

Over thirty other names for American ethnic groups derive from historical associations, literary allusions, folklore, and the popular culture of the mass media.

By way of historical associations, African Americans in the 1920s and 1930s were called both *Marcus* and *Garvey*, from the name of the separatist leader. By the early nineteenth century, Dutch descendants in New York were indiscriminately called *Knickerbockers*, from the name of Diedrich Knickerbocker, the fictitious author of Washington Irving's *History of New York*. The Japanese and sometimes Japanese Americans during the Second World War were called *Tojo*, after General Hideki Tojo. *House-of-David Boy*, a derisive name for Jews, is of course a biblical reference. An old, borrowed name for the Swiss is *Colin Tampon*, which might allude to the drum roll of the Swiss Guard. U. S. Southerners have been called *Jeff* and *Jeff Davis*, from the name Jefferson Davis, President of the Confederate States of America. Germans were called *Turners*, which only mimics a personal name, because it is from *Turnverein*, the German-American fraternal and athletic societies, whose members were called "Turners." In the early decades of this century, a German was sometimes called a *Hohenzollern*, from the name of the former royal family. Germans were also called *Cousin Michael*, from *der deutsche Michel*, the German peasantry.

By way of literary allusions, *Sambo* for blacks, which possibly derives from a Hausan personal name meaning "second son," was popularized again in recent times by Helen Bannerman's famous 1930 children's story, *The Little Black Sambo Story Book*. *Uncle Remus*, which became a popular nickname for older black men, is the character in the stories by Joel Chandler Harris. In the late nineteenth century, *Liza* or *Lize* became a common nickname for a black girl or woman; H. L. Mencken (1963) said the name was "apparently a reminiscence of 'Uncle Tom's Cabin'." (*Eliza* was the name of the black woman who, with her infant, was pursued over the ice floes of the Ohio River.) Native Americans were sometimes nicknamed *Hiawatha*, and Jews, *Shylock*. *Pinocchio*, a recent nickname for an Italian, is the name of the puppet in Carlo Lorenzini's fairy tale. *John Bull*, the personification of the English, also became *Johnny Bull*, a derisive nickname for an Englishman, both deriving from the title of Arbuthnot's 1712 allegory, *The History of John Bull*. *Joan Bull* is a recent feminization.

Folklore is the source of several terms. *Johnny Cake* for French Canadians, according to Abraham A. Roback, derives from a children's doggerel in Montreal's Protestant schools around 1900: "French peasoup and Johnny cake / Make your father a bellyache." *Hans Wurst* for Germans is from the name of the buffoon in German folk plays since 1600. *Speedy Gonzalez* for a Mexican derives from the name of the rapacious hero of the ethnic jokes. *Buttinski* for a Jew, or for any intrusive person, probably comes from stereotypical beliefs about the oral assertiveness of Jews; the *-ski* is from the ending of the Slavic surnames of many Eastern Jews.

The popular culture of the mass media, beginning with minstrelsy, is a larger and still vital source of ethnic epithets, especially in black and white relations. Minstrel songs popularized a few names for African Americans. H. L. Mencken relates these, including the case of *coon* discussed in chapter 1. *Jim Crow*, from *crow*, an earlier term for blacks, was introduced by Thomas D. Rice's 1828 dance and song "Jim Crow," which contained the line "My name's Jim Crow." *Rastus* was a popular nickname for blacks in the 1880s, and it was made even more popular by "Rastus on Parade," an 1896 song by Kerry Mills. A few others are obvious. *Old Black Joe* was popularized if not introduced by the 1860 Stephen Foster song of that title. *Aunt Jemima* was popularized in 1876 by the minstrel song "Old Aunt Jemima," and later it was surely influenced by the brand name of the pancake mix. *Abie Kabbibble* for a Jew is from the character in Harry Hershfield's popular comic strip, "Abie the Agent," which ran from 1914 to 1940.

The recent popular culture of radio, movies, and television inspired other names. *Buckwheat* for blacks derives from the historical idea that blacks ate buckwheat as a staple, but the name was certainly reinforced by the name of Buckwheat Thomas, the child actor in the "Our Gang" movie series. *Sapphire* for a black woman was inspired by the namesake character on the "Amos and Andy" radio and television programs. *Goldberg*, a name that urban blacks in the 1960s used for Jews who employed black domestics, was also earlier a stereotypical name for Jews. But it was surely reinforced, though inaccurately, by the character of Mrs. Goldberg of radio and television fame. *Mickey Mouse* and *Sylvester*, the latter from Mel Blanc's ridiculous cartoon cat character, are black names for whites. *Little Eva* was a name for a loudmouth white girl; the origin is not known to me.

NAMES THOUGHT COMMON IN GROUPS

The final class of over a hundred personal names that became stereotypes for ethnic persons is mostly given names that outsiders thought were especially common in a group. Blacks, Jews, and Mexicans have accumulated the largest numbers, though this particular stereotyping device has been used for eighteen other groups. I will discuss the names for each target group.

African American men were stereotyped with the names *George, James, Leroy,* and *Moses*. In particular, *George*, according to Stuart Berg Flexner in *Listening to America* (1982),

was used from the 1880s as a term of address for any Pullman car porter, either because it was such a common name
for black men or because of the association with George
Pullman, who invented the Pullman car and who decided to
staff the sleepers solely with black porters.

A few generic names for black men probably originated
as West African given names, became known in this country
as names of slaves, and later were applied loosely to any
black man. *Cuffee* or *Cuffy* was recorded in 1713 and was
used for blacks down to the 1880s, and was also shortened
to *Cuff*. Linguist J. L. Dillard (1976) says that the name derives from the West African day name, *Cuffee*, for a male
child born on Friday. Similarly, *Quashee, -ie*, recorded in the
1840s, derives from Ashanti *Quashee*, a male child born on
Sunday. The variant *Squasho* appeared about 1900. *Sambo*
possibly derives from a given name in several West African
languages, according to linguist David Dalby (1972).

Black women were slightingly nicknamed *Lize, Liza*, and
Lizzie (from *Elizabeth*). In *Listening to America*, Flexner writes
that *Elizabeth* "was such a common black first name it was
used by whites from the 1880s until the late 1920s as a
generic word to refer to any black woman, especially a black
servant, as a cook or maid. Early in this century, whites even
joked that black domestics had *Elizabeth clubs* on their day
off to gossip about their employers, compare wages and
working conditions, etc." Flexner also says that the name *tin
lizzie* for the Model T Ford (which Henry Ford said was
available in "any color as long as it's black") may well be
from the nickname for a black maid; the car, like the maid,
"worked hard all week and prettied up on Sunday."

Black women were also generically called *Mandy* (from
Amanda). *Peola* also has been listed as a generic name for a
black woman. *Peola* may derive from a given name—at least
it is the name of the daughter of a black woman in the movie
Imitation of Life, released in 1934. I found *Juba* listed in one
source as a generic name for a black woman. *Juba* was a

common given name for black girls, and Flexner in *Listening to America* notes that the proper name derives from the West African day name for a girl born on Monday.

Irish personal names seem especially apt to be made generic. The most variously turned is *Pat*, from *Patrick*, which was a popular given name. *Pat* was variegated to *Patty*, *Patlander*, and, for women, *Patess*. Closely related is *Paddy*, from *Padraig*, the Gaelic form of *Patrick*. *Paddy* was variegated to *Paddylander* and *Paddyw(h)ack*. These names became so famous as generic names for the Irish that blacks extended their meaning and made them generic for all whites. Blacks have called whites *Paddy*, *Paddy Boy*, *Patty*, *Patty Boy*, and *White Paddy*. Another black term for whites is *Dap*, backslang from *Pad*, from *Paddy*. (Another black name for whites, *Honky*, a dialectal black pronunciation of *Hunky*, the old slur for an East or Central European immigrant, is a similar extension to all whites, though it is not formed on a personal name.)

The nicknames for any Irishman that derive from *Michael*, including *Michael* itself, are as well known. *Mike* was a generic name for any Irishman, but *Mick* and *Mickey* were more offensive and appeared in the slurs *Whiskey Mick* and *Cheap Shanty Mick*. John Ciardi (1980) says that *Mickey Finn* also is generic for an Irishman. In the nineteenth century, Mexicans were sometimes called *Micks*, for the term was generalized to several despised, low-status groups, perhaps especially if they were Roman Catholic. (As in the cases of *Pat* and *Paddy*, *Mickey* has become a black term for whites, probably also influenced by Walt Disney's Mickey Mouse and the slang idea of *mickey mouse* as trivial work.) Other nicknames for Irishmen derive from given names: *Ted* and *Teddy* from *Theodore*, and *Tad* from *Thaddeus*. For women, *Bridget* and its diminutive *Biddy* were used. Ciardi says *Biddy* probably derives from a British baby-talk rendering of *Bridget*, finally becoming *Bidgie* and *Biddy*.

Several nicknames for the Irish derive from family names,

such as *Dogan*, *Donovan*, *Mulligan*, *Murphy* (often shortened
to *Murph* and burlesqued to *Moiphy*), and *Teague*. *Mac(k)*
for any Irishman comes from the prefix of many Irish surnames, and for the same reason *Mac(k)* is also a popular
name for Scots.

Other British Isles groups were called names that were
based on personal names. Scotsmen have been called *Mac(k)*
more often than the Irish. *Sandy* is a familiar form of *Alex-
ander*, and *Sawney* is a variant of *Sandy*. Scotsmen were also
nicknamed *MacTavish* and *Saunders*. The Welsh were called
Taffy (and *Taffy Mouth*), from the sound of the Welsh *Daf-
fydd*, i.e., *David* (as *Davy*), a common given name and a so-
briquet for St. David, the patron saint of Wales. Welsh
women in the United States were called *Cousin Ann*, a feminine counterpart of *Cousin Jack*. (Cornishmen in the United
States were also called *Cousin Jack*, and Cornish women,
Cousin Jenny.)

Most of the names for Jews derive from given names,
though the family names *Levi*, *Goldberg* and *Goldstein* have
been used. The following given names have been recorded
as slurs when used generically: *Abe* and *Abie* (from *Abraham*), *Dave*, *Hymie* (from *Hyman*), *Ikey*, and *Ike* (from *Isaac*),
Ikey-Mo (from a blend of *Ikey* and *Mo*, from *Moses*), *Izzy* (from
Isidore), *Jake* (from *Jacob*), *Max*, *Moses*, *Mouchey* (perhaps from
Moishe, i.e., *Moses*), *Sol* (from *Solomon*). *Sammy* is from *Samuel*, and see my discussion of the generic *Sammy* under terms
that connote low status and anonymity. For women, *Rachel*
and *Rebecca* similarly were used. *Rebecca*, in particular, was
further influenced by the character, Rebecca, the daughter
of Isaac of York, in Sir Walter Scott's novel *Ivanhoe*, which
was immensely popular in this country in the nineteenth
century and was mandatory schoolroom reading well into
this century.

The slur *dago*, from the Spanish and Portuguese given name
Diego, James, was attached to Italians by the late nineteenth
century, though it was earlier used for the Spanish and the

Portuguese and, rarely, for Mexicans. Other generic names for Italians are *Carlo* and *Tony*, from, and also, *Antonio*. Fred Tarpley, the well-known dialectologist at East Texas State University, reported *poppie squalie* (1970, p. 250) from Northeast Texas; possibly it is from the sound of *Pasquale*. *Dino*, a diminutive of *Constantino*, was used for Italian men, as well as for Mexicans and other groups associated with low-status labor, when it was sometimes spelled *Dyno*.

Hispanic men have been called *Pedro* (Mexicans and Puerto Ricans), *Felipe* (Mexicans in Los Angeles), *José* (Spaniards), and *Don* (Portuguese, and from the title before some Portuguese surnames). *Chico*, a common nickname from Spanish *chico*, little boy, has been used for Mexicans, Puerto Ricans, and even Filipinos.

German immigrants in the United States have been called *Fritz* and *Fritzie*, *-y*, *Heiney* (from *Heinrich*), and *Hans* (cf. *Hans Wurst*, a name for Germans derived from a folkloristic allusion). Young women were slightingly referred to as *Gretchen*. Dutchmen were called *Hans*, also a common given name in Holland, *Closh*, from *Claus*, and with mock respect, *Mijnheer Closh*. Dutchmen have also been called *Nic(k) Frog*, where *Nic(k)* is from *Nicholas* and *Frog* from *Frogland(er)*, a dweller in lowlands where frogs abound.

A variety of other European groups have one or two stereotypical names derived from personal names. *Horwat* was noted in 1919 to apply to any Hungarian. Lee Pederson, the noted dialectologist at Emory University, reported in 1964 that *Stashu* (i.e., *Stanley*) was used for Poles in Chicago. *Olaf* and *Ole* were used for Swedes. *Abdul* was a ridiculing name for any Turk. Russians are still called *Ivan* and, with mock formality, *Ivan Ivanovitch*. The *-ich* suffix on many Slavic surnames caused Serbs and Croats to be called *Itch*, *Itchy*, and irresistibly *Itchy-coo*.

Blacks have used several generic names for whites, which are formed on personal names. I discussed above the *Charlie* and *Mister Charlie* complex of names. Blacks also called whites *Mister Eddie, Mister Jones, Fred,* and *Herbie. Miss Anne* and *Miss Annie* are names for a white woman, especially one in a position of authority. Whites, perhaps only white women, in the South were sometimes called *Gillian,* which possibly derives from the identical informal name for *Juliana. Gillian* for *Juliana* somehow came to mean a "wench." I note, too, that *Gillie, -ey,* and *Giles* were nineteenth-century slang for a stupid person.

Finally, Brewton Berry (1963), the sociologist, reports that eleven generic names for residents of isolated, racially mixed communities are derived from family names thought common in these groups. About two hundred such communities of people of various Indian, white, and black mixes are in the eastern United States, or were at least until recent decades. Social scientists call them "Tri-Racial Isolates." Berry speculates that the name *Pools* for one such group derives from the surname *Vanderpool; Males* may derive from *Mayle, Mail,* or *Mahle; Creels* from *Creel; Chavises* from *Chavis; Collinses* from *Collins; Coe-clan* from *Coe; Bones* from *Boone* (though it might be from *redbones,* an epithet for a racially mixed person); *Goins,* he speculates, is also from the surname. The *VanGuilder(s),* the *Laster Tribe,* and the *Clapper(s)* each derive from those family names.

Personal names that became ethnic epithets show some of the origins of intergroup name-calling in cultural clashes. Prejudice grows out of conflictful relations that draw into relief cultural differences between groups. The particulars of these differences, such as personal names, become the stuff of name-calling.

CHAPTER 4

MEN . . . AND ONE HUNDRED EPITHETS FOR ETHNIC WOMEN

THIS CHAPTER REVIEWS and lists more than one hundred ethnic slurs that historically have been used against women of twenty different ethnic groups. These words, as their substance will soon make apparent, originate in both gender and ethnic conflict. The ethnic stereotypes carried by these terms of abuse indicate the pejorative images that most often have been used against ethnic women, as well as indicating the groups that most often have been abused with these words. Only a few of these pejorative names that men called women could be construed to be neutral to positive in sentiment, even considering all the possible situations that modified their meaning in actual use.

MALE SEX ROLES, ANXIETY, AND SLANG

Terms of abuse for ethnic women are chiefly a male vocabulary of slang. Slang in general also is mainly a male vocabulary, and its social referents tend to be stressful relations of all kinds. This prompts an elucidating analogy. Ethnic slurs in general bear a relation to ethnic conflicts and anxieties similar to that which words of sexual insult and sexually "dirty" words bear to stressful relations between men and women.

Ethnic abuse is one of the most frequent social topics in American slang, growing out of ethnic conflict and reflecting the great diversity of American society. Much ethnic conflict is a result of economic conflict, especially in male work roles and struggles over status hierarchies. In a similar way, the thousands of derogatory words for women, their bodies, and sexual acts of all kinds reflect the stresses and anxieties of traditional male sex roles. Each vocabulary is preeminently a political vocabulary that seeks to exert social control, to maintain privilege, and generally to wield power.

Ethnic slurs in general are also a semantic parallel with the abusive language that men have used against women. Comparing the work of such linguists as Roger W. Wescott (1971) on the sound semantics of ethnic slurs with that of Ethel Strainchamps (1971) and of Casey Miller and Kate Swift (1977) on the sound semantics of sexual slurs strongly suggests a connection. Ethnic epithets, as a vocabulary of psychological aggression, share with gender epithets clusters of phonetic elements, such as popping and gutteral sounds, whose sound semantics perhaps universally or at least widely connote pejoration.

Terms for ethnic women, the intersection of the two vocabularies, spring from the dual anxieties—and subsequent aggressions—fostered by ethnic conflict, on the one hand, and traditional male sex roles with respect to women, on the other. These terms derogate both ethnic and sex roles, each by the other, and are particularly revealing of the historical quality of these relations.

THE TARGETS AND ALLUSIONS OF
THE WORDS

These terms of abuse are chiefly interracial and most are directed at women of racial minorities. Four times as many terms refer to black as to white women. Some twenty terms for women of other racial minorities refer to Native American, Asian, and Pacific groups. Most terms for Asian and Pacific groups originated in military slang during foreign wars.

Some of the terms are mild. About a dozen, for example, derive from stereotypical given names thought common in the group, such as *Liza* for blacks, *Gretchen* for Germans, *Bridget* for the Irish, and *Rachel* for Jewish women. But many more terms allude to stereotypical physical traits of ethnic groups and deal in sexual insult.

Of the interracial terms, about four in ten allude to physical differences. Almost all the interracial terms using physical stereotypes were used between blacks and whites. A single word can have multiple allusions, combining perhaps a color reference and gender insult in the same term, such as the puns *raven beauty*, *shady lady*, and *white meat*. Ruth Todasco (1973) compiled an inventory of derogatory words for women in general, which shows that many trade heavily in animal metaphors and in the identity of female genitalia with women themselves. Words for ethnic women reflect the same themes. At least one in five terms are highly derogatory allusions to women's bodies and otherwise deride their sexuality. Most of the terms display, not surprisingly, the historical male inclination to depersonalize women as anonymous sex objects. A few of the words equate ethnic women with genitalia, such as *black cunt*, *poontang*, and perhaps *scuttle sault* and *pale sault*. A few words identify ethnic women with prostitution, such as *poontang*, *skibby*, and perhaps *gin*, supposedly her preferred drink.

Some of the words combine bizarre allusions to sexuality and food, such as *brown sugar*, *dark meat* (and *white meat*), *chocolate drop*, *honey*, *hot chocolate*, *fortune-cookie*, *frog legs*, *hot tamale*, *mexican dish*, and perhaps *pineapple*. Stuart Berg Flexner in his preface to the *Dictionary of American Slang* (1975) notes the prominence of food references in slang and, further, the "subconscious" relating of sex and food, as in *banana*, *cheese cake*, *cherry*, *jelly roll*, *meat*, *cookie*, *peach*, *quail*, *tomato*, and of course *dish*, where you can have a *Mexican dish* or one of most any nationality. Speculations on the deep meaning of this association might be endless. It is enough to say that slang terms for ethnic women share this trait with American slang generally.

Another trait that terms for ethnic women share both with ethnic epithets in general and with terms of abuse for women in general is the use of animal metaphors. These metaphors also overlap with other allusions: *raven beauty, seal, monkey Jane, bitch, frog legs, moose*, and perhaps *gooney gal*. Also another device connotes animalism. Pejoration is often done or increased with suffixes and modifiers. One morphemic element with an unfavorable connotation is the suffix *-ess* to make a name gratuitously feminine, such as *heebess, jewess, niggeress*, and *patess*. This device, which is otherwise used to feminize words for roles that are normatively male, also connotes an animal metaphor, for the same suffix is used to feminize the names of animals, such as *lioness* and *tigress*.

Another order of words, in addition to those listed in the glossary, includes several that were used for racially mixed women, mostly women of black and white parentage. One of the oldest terms is *métisse*, the feminine of Louisiana French *métis*, mongrel, half-breed, which was a loanword in American English by the 1790s. *Mulatress*, in this feminine form, appeared at the beginning of the nineteenth century (from *mulatto*, ultimately from Portuguese and Spanish *mulato*, diminutive of *mulo*, a mule). The following are later terms marked by sources as applying especially to women: *banana; bird's eye maple; high yellow* (dialectally pronounced *-yeller* and *-yaller*); *lemon; peola* (perhaps a given name); *pink toes; pinky, -ie* (a usage reflected in Elia Kazan's 1949 movie *Pinky*, whose title role was played by Jeanne Crain); *redbone*; and *yellow girl* (1860s).

HISTORICAL GLOSSARY OF SLUR-NAMES FOR ETHNIC WOMEN

The following word list, which is arranged by ethnic group, is a virtually complete historical inventory of recorded epithets for ethnic women in American slang. About a fifth of all historical ethnic slurs are gender specific, referring either to men or women. About half of the fifth refer specifically to women. All these words, which have accumulated since the colonial period down to the present, can be found in scholarly records of American slang and other informal speech. Most of the terms are obsolete, though a few are occasionally heard today. Some of the terms, chiefly the older words, are dated for their first appearance in American printed texts. Most of the undated words are probably of late nineteenth- and twentieth-century origins. I have given etymologies when these are not self-evident.

Black or African-American Women

aunt   Early 1830s. Also *auntie, -y*. Used for older women.

Aunt Jemima   From a nineteenth-century minstrel song. Later reinforced by the name of the "Aunt Jemima" brand of pancake mix.

bitch   Probably nineteenth century. Often *black bitch*.

bit of ebony   Nineteenth century. Ebony is a dark wood from the Old World and a valuable importation, as were slaves.

black cunt

black doll

black mama

brown sugar   Also *sugar brown*, inverted in the folk manner.

charcoal blossom   Also *charcoal lily*.

coal   A particularly derogatory allusion to dark color.

chocolate drop   1912. Also *sweet chocolate*.

covess dinge   1850. From the feminine form of *cove*, an old slang term for a fellow, and *dinge*, a term for a black person.

cullud gal   A Southern dialectal, later burlesqued, rendering of *colored girl*.

dange broad   From the old adjective *dange*, sexy.

dark meat   Also *piece of dark meat, rare piece of dark meat, hot piece of dark meat*.

dusky dame   Once a popular alliterative form.

femoke   Probably from *fem* or *femme*, a slang term for a woman, and *moke*, a term for any black person.

gin   Originally a prostitute. Perhaps for *gin*, the liquor, folklorically her preferred drink.

honey   A food reference, but perhaps also an allusion to light skin color.

hot chocolate   An allusion to both color and sexuality.

Indian princess   A "euphemism" for a black woman.

jigaboo   In carnival slang, usually feminine.

jit   Usually feminine. From *jitney*, a five-cent piece, hence anything of small value.

Juba   From the West African day name for a girl born on Monday.

Liza   Late nineteenth century. Also *Lize, Lizzie*, all from *Elizabeth*.

laundry queen   An allusion to the role of domestic service, or to taking in wash.

mammy   Late nineteenth century. Also rendered *maumer*. Used for older women, especially nursemaids.

Mandy   From the given name *Amanda*.

mocha   Usually feminine. Probably from *mocha*, for its color. Mocha is a blend of coffee and chocolate.

monkey Jane   1920s.

negress   The traditional but by early in this century gratuitous feminine form of *negro*.

niggeress   A compounding of the slur.

nigger gal

Peola Possibly from a personal name. See chapter 3.

poontang 1870s. From Louisiana French, *putain*, whore.

raven beauty A pun on the *g*-less pronunciation of *ravin' beauty*.

Sapphire From a supposedly common given name, popularized by a character in the "Amos and Andy" radio and television series.

scuttle sault *Scuttle* alludes to a coal scuttle and *sault* is perhaps an old slang term for a woman, as an instance of sexual intercourse. Cf. *pale sault*, a black term for a white woman.

seal Usually feminine. An allusion to the dark color and sleek coat of the marine animal.

shady lady A pun on *shade*, a term for any black person.

saucer lip Also *ubangi*.

wench 1765. Often *negro-* or *nigger wench*.

woman of color[1] Late eighteenth century. Also *lady of color*.

Chinese Women

Chinawoman 1872. *China* used as an adjective in this form is now thought offensive, as is *Chinaman*.

ching doll *Ching* is a nineteenth-century name for Chinese person.

fortune cookie The light dessert is also an American invention.

segoonya Second World War. Reportedly derived from a Chinese word. But possibly it is an alteration of German *Zigeuner* (feminine *Zigeunerin*), gypsy or tramp, which is a rough sound parallel. English *Tzigane* and cognates in several other languages derive from Hungarian *Cigány*.

slopie gal From *slope*, *slopie*, all from *slope head*, a term for any Chinese.

Cornish Women

Cousin Jenny Counterpart of masculine *Cousin Jack*. *Cousin Jack* is more often used for the Welsh in the United States.

English Women

Joan Bull   A modern variant of *John Bull*, or England personified.

Inupiat, Inuit, or Eskimo Women

esquaw   Perhaps from a variant of Algonquian *squa*, a woman, hence *squaw*, or a blend of *Es*kimo and *squaw*.

esquimuff   Perhaps an alteration of *Eskimo* or Canadian French *Esquimau* or perhaps a blend of *Eskimo* and *muff*, which has been a slang term for a woman and for female genitalia, and it is the name of a type of fur mitten.

squaw   An extension of the usually disparaging name for any Native American woman, originally from the Algonquian languages, first recorded in 1634.

Filipino Women

phillipean   Or *philipeen*. Certainly influenced by sound and spelling of *Philippine* and *Filipino*. But, I conjecture, it is also from the unrelated *philopena*, *fillipeen*, *phillipina*, etc., which were all late nineteenth-century altered, Anglicized forms of German *Vielliebchen*, darling, sweetheart. Possibly originated, in this application, in the Spanish-American War.

French Women

frog legs   A multi-layered and graphic pun on *frog* for any French person.

German Women

Gretchen   From the popular given name.

Fräulein   The German word for a young, unmarried girl or woman.

Irish Women

Bridget Also the diminutive *biddy*. From the popular given name.

girleen Diminutive of *girl*.

Patess A feminine form of the generic nickname *Pat*, from *Patrick*, the popular given name for men.

Japanese Women

cherry blossom Probably from the fame of cherry trees in Japanese gardens and in Washington, D. C. and a pun on the slang term *cherry*, a young female virgin.

geisha Offensive when misapplied to a Japanese-American woman.

skibby 1910–20. Perhaps originally a female prostitute, later applied to any Japanese. Perhaps from Japanese *sukebei*, lewdness, lechery. It may have been heard as a salutation of prostitutes and the corrupted word was applied to them. Cf. *geisha*.

Jewish Women

bagel baby 1960s. Especially, a young woman interested in liberal causes.

ghettess Around 1900. From the noun *ghetto*.

Jewess The once traditional and acceptable form is now considered gratuitous and offensive.

heebess A burlesque of *Hebrewess*, another epithet.

JAP An acronym for *Jewish American Princess*. See chapter 9. A gross stereotype and offensive.

Rachel From the given name.

Rebecca From the given name. Nineteenth century.

zaftig Or *zoftig*. 1940. From nearly identical German and Yiddish adjectives, meaning plump, well-rounded, buxom. Non-Yiddish speakers have used it as a noun and slur-name.

Korean Women

moose   Originally a female prostitute, but later applied to any girl or woman. Perhaps from Japanese *musume*, girl. Yet *moose* is American slang for an "ugly" woman.

slant eye   The generic slur for any Asian person seemed to become chiefly feminine when referring to Koreans.

Mexican Women

hot tamale   1929. Also a pun on slang *hot*, sexy.

mexican dish   1930s. A pun on slang *dish*, an attractive woman.

sexy mex(y)

Native American Women

squaw   From various Algonquian words for *woman*. Later used for any Native American woman. See under Inupiat Women.

Pacific-Islander Women

gee chee   Often feminine. Perhaps from either Japanese *geisha*, a female entertainer, or *geechee*, a Bahamian black person. It is also a generic term for a Eurasian woman.

gooney gal   Also *gooney girl*. From *gooney*, a term of uncertain origin for any South Seas Islander, but possibly from the name of the gooney bird.

grass skirt   A Hawaiian. A pun on slang *skirt*, a woman.

hula Lula   Also *hulahula*. A Hawaiian. Cf. *grass skirt*.

Mary   Originally any female household servant. From the given name.

pineapple   A native "dish."

shack mammy   Related to slang *to shack up*, to live illicitly with a local woman in a tropical "shack."

squack   Origin not known to me, but clearly a sound derogation.

wahini, wahine, or **vahine**   Hawaiian or Moari.

Russian Women

steppe sister   A pun on *stepsister* and the Russian *Steppes.*

Southern Women

southern belle   Also *belle.* The famous ethnic stereotype.

rebel   World War Two Army slang for a Southern young woman. From much older *rebel,* a Southerner or Confederate soldier.

Southern-Highlander Women

hillnelly   Modeled on *hillbilly.* From the given name *Nelly,* diminutive of *Nell,* once thought common in the hills.

Welsh Women

Cousin Ann   Originally the wife of a Welsh miner working in the United States and the feminine counterpart of *Cousin Jack,* a Welshman.

White Women (used by black men)

bale of straw   Also *straw.* An allusion to straighter, sometimes blonde hair.

blondie   A reference to lighter hair and complexion.

Charlene   A term apparently chosen because it is cognate with *Charlie,* as in *Mister Charlie.* Probably 1960s.

golden girl   Again, "golden" hair and blonde complexion.

grey broad   From *grey* or *gray,* a black term for a white person.

Miss Anne   1940s. Also *Miss Annie.* Expressed a sentiment similar to *Charlene.* The variants *Miss Amy,* for a young white girl, and *Miss Lillian,* for an older white woman, appeared in

Los Angeles in the early 1970s, and both are obviously from the names of Amy Carter and Lillian Carter, the daughter and late mother of President Jimmy Carter.

pale sault   Cf. *scuttle sault*, a white term for a black woman. The meaning of *sault* is unclear but it may be a sexual allusion.

pearls   Also *stars*.

pinkie, -y   From *pink*, a black term for a white person.

pink toes   Down to her toes. Also diminutive in intent.

silk broad   *Silk* is an allusion to finer, straighter hair.

white-meat   1930s, but probably earlier. Compare *dark-meat* under Black or African-American Women.

NOTE

1. *Women of color,* semantically inverted, is becoming acceptable to denote generically women of several traditionally oppressed minority groups in the United States. The expression seems to be an avoidance of the equally generic but implicitly pejorative term *nonwhite* (see pages 80–81). Yet I hear less often the phrase *people of color* and only rarely *men of color.*

CHAPTER 5

YOU ARE WHAT YOU EAT: DIETARY STEREOTYPES

WHEREVER ETHNIC GROUPS meet and come into conflict, they usually call one another names to disparage highly visible cultural differences, such as crude stereotypes of dietary customs and related practices. About one in fourteen ethnic epithets in historical American slang is a dietary stereotype. The smorgasbord in the pages that follow arranges these derisive nicknames by their food referents, soup to nuts.

FOOD REFERENTS

Soup. Americans borrowed the Continental and British slur *Jean potage* for our immigrant French. But immigrant Quebeckers were a more visible group, and their staple pea-soup by the 1890s resulted in *Johnny peasoup* and the popular variants *peasoup*, *pea souper*, and *French peasoup*. Their pea soup is probably the allusion in *pea-eye*. German Americans were called *metzel*, deriving I speculate from *Metzelsuppe* or metzel soup, made with sausage, and a popular dish in nineteenth-century immigrant communities.

Seafood. Several groups have been nicknamed for doing

violence to herring and mackerel. Swedes and Norwegians were variously called *herring snapper* and *herring destroyer*. Jews were derided with *herring punisher* and *lox jock*. Roman Catholics were tagged with *mackerel snapper* (and *mackerel snatcher*), *fish eater*, and alliteratively, *guppy gobbler*. (The Catholic kids then called their Protestant tormenters *cheese eater*, an old euphemism for *rat* and which later had scatological allusions). *Conch*, from the name of the edible gastropod, is an old name for a poor black or white Bahamian and for a white on the lower east coast of Florida. Today the nickname is best known as the proud moniker for a native of Key West, Florida—mostly whites.

Frog and Its Variants. *Frog* is the only ethnic epithet whose modern use was influenced by a culinary delicacy—frog legs. The English thought the French taste for frog legs was bizarre and loathsome, and more than a century ago began calling the French *frog eater*, *frog*, *froggy*, and the like. We borrowed these Britishisms and especially after the First World War applied them to French immigrants, Quebeckers in the United States, and their distant relatives, the Acadians in Louisiana. A cute pig-Latin *ogfray* was sometimes heard, probably as a schoolboy's slur. A French child, irresistibly, was called a *tadpole*. Young French women were sometimes called *frog legs*, obviously a pun, but also evoking a vivid image of spread and kicking legs. Though perhaps only as in the can-can dance.

Some scholars, such as John Ciardi (1980), show evidence that *frog* did not derive from the eating of frog legs at all but from the image of saltant toads on the coats of arms of early French kings, the shape of the *fleur de lis*, and other early representations. We borrowed another, related Britishism for the French, *crapaud*, French for toad. It is probably true that *frog* ultimately derives from the image of the *crapaud* on things French, but the eating of frog legs surely influenced the nickname and kept it kicking. French and French Canadian immigrants in this country were called *cra-*

paud, *Jean crapaud*, and *Johnny crapaud*. And *crapaud* was often pronounced "crappo" and "crow-poo" to garnish the loathsome frog.

Pasta. Italians have long been called *spaghetti* and the variants *spaghetti bender*, *spaghetti eater*, *speg eater*, *spaghetti head*, and *spaghet*. On top of all this spaghetti is a *meatball*, an Italian. *Spaghetti* was shortened to *spag* and then perhaps thinned to *spig*. *Spiggoty* is from *spig* or from the sound of *spaghetti*. Early in this century, *spig* was variegated to *spic* or *spick* and was applied to a variety of other groups, mostly Latin Americans, especially Mexicans. The famous story about "No spicka de Engleesh" probably just reinforced the usage. Italians were also called *macaroni*, which has been a symbol of Italianate things since the eighteenth century. Recently, Italians have been called *macaroni smackers*. *Macaroni* is also slang for a dude or fop, and lately a name for a black pimp. In Yiddish-American slang, an Italian was a *lukshen* and *loksh*, Yiddish for noodle, i.e., spaghetti.

Other Cereals. Jews were called *Jew bagel*, *bagel bender*, and just *bagel*, as well as *motzo*, *motzer*, and sometimes *motzey*. In the 1960s in New York, middle-class young Jewish women who flocked to liberal causes were called *bagel babies*. Blacks were called *buckwheat*, as mentioned in chapter 3, from the popular historical association of blacks eating buckwheat. The term served in the early 1980s as a comic name for a black character in a skit on television's "Saturday Night Live." *Pancake*, and there are buckwheat pancakes, was among blacks an ingroup slur for an "Uncle Tom." This nexus might have been influenced, moreover, by the "Aunt Jemima" brand of pancake mixes, which includes a buckwheat mix. The Chinese were called *rice belly* and, in black street slang, *ricer* and *rice man*. In New York the new Korean immigrants and probably other Asian groups are sometimes called *eggrolls*. In L. A. Mexicans have been called *tostado*.

Cornmeal in New World ethnic diets is the source of names for several groups. *Cracker* is a name for certain ethnic

Southerners, especially Georgians, and it is a black name for whites, especially those thought to be racists. According to the scholar Delma E. Presley (1976), *cracker*, which dates from 1784, has an uncertain etymology, though possibly it is from the practice of early, mostly Scotch-Irish settlers eating cracked corn. *Cracker* is possibly short for *corn cracker*, which was a name for a Southern highlander in the nineteenth century.

The prominence of cornmeal in the diets of Mexican peasants is reflected in *enchilada eater*, *tortilla eater*, *taco*, *taco eater*, *taco head*, *taco bender*, and *tamale*. The "Anglo" boys in the Southwest in the 1920s and 1930s drooled over young Mexican-American women with the witless puns *hot tamale* and *Mexican dish*. The Chicanos adapted the blacks' ingroup slur, *Uncle Tom*, for a Spanish cornmeal version, *Tio Taco*, which serves alongside the more parallel *Tio Tomás*. Far to the north, French Canadians were called *Johnny cake*. In New York City the many German settlers in the nineteenth century were called *pretzels* from their reputation as bakers as well as eaters of the knotted glazed and salted cracker.

Condiments. Mexican Americans, as far as I can determine, are the only group that has been nicknamed for the condiments in their diet. By about 1920, the name *pepper* was fairly common and soon variegated to *pepper gut*, *pepper belly*, and *hot pepper belly*. One of the peppers, of course, is chili, and Mexicans have also been dubbed *chili*, *chili bean*, *chili eater*, *chili belly*, and alliteratively *chili chomper* and *chili choker*.

Tubers, Roots, and Legumes. The Irish were called *potato eater*, *potato head*, and *spud*, and the French Canadians are still sometimes slurred with *frit* and *French fries*. Groups as disparate as Mexicans and Yankees, especially Bostonians, have been called *bean eater*. The bean theme for Mexicans has been variegated to *bean*, *beaner*, *beano*, *bean choker*, *bean eater*, and *frijole guzzler*. In and around the state of Utah, Mormons have been called *carrot-eaters* or *carrot-snappers*.

Butter and Cheese. *Buttermouth* and *butterbox* are old slurs on the Dutch. Hollanders in the seventeenth century and earlier were called *Jan Kaas*, "John Cheese." As told in chapter 3, *Jan Kaas* was also applied briefly to the Dutch of New York and later was somehow turned on the English of Connecticut, where it stuck and emerged as *Yankees*. Germans, for a while after 1904, were called *limburger*, sometimes spelled and pronounced *limberger*, which was shortened to *limberg*. Blacks sometimes called rural Southern whites *buttermilk swallower*, possibly because at one time buttermilk was considered not fit for human consumption and slopped to the hogs.

Cabbage. *Cabbage head* after 1854 was applied to both the Dutch and Germans in the United States. The name of any vegetable that is big, round, and seemingly solid is apt to be used as an ethnic slur. (New England Yankees were once called *pumpkin head*.) Since 1904, Germans have been called *sauerkraut*. Since the First World War, they have been called *kraut*, and, since the Second World War *krauthead* and *kraut eater*. Russians were named *cabbage eater*, as well as *kraut eater*.

Red Meats. The English, probably in this century, came to be called *beefeaters*, probably from the dual influence of the fame of English roast beef and the name of the warders of the Tower of London, the Beefeaters.[1] Germans have been long associated with making sausage and were called *wurst* and *sausage*. The old personification, *Hans Wurst*, rarely was used in American English; Hans Wurst was the traditional buffoon in German folk plays since 1600. *Pork chop* seems to be a general term of status disparagement and has been applied to several low-status minorities. *Pork chop* and *porker* have been used for Jews, of course, precisely because the name callers were aware of the dietary prohibition. Much earlier in the American colonial period North Carolinians were called *porkers* because of their dietary habit. In the black street slang of Los Angeles, a white person was sometimes called *swine eater*, a term possibly influenced by knowledge of the dietary prohibition among black Muslims. (On the other hand, the almost ritual serving of chicken dinners at church socials apparently got Methodists the name of *chicken eaters*.) Hungarians are nicknamed *goulash*—the stew of beef, veal, and vegetables. Rural blacks were called *possum*, from *opossum*, supposedly from hunting or eating them.

One proper name for an ethnic group, *Eskimo*, derives from a dietary stereotype. *Eskimo*, by way of French *Esquimau*, is ultimately from an Algonquian word meaning "eater of raw meat" and was an ethnic epithet used by Native Canadian Indian groups. Eskimo groups often prefer to be called by their own names for themselves, such as *Inupiat* and *Inuit*, meaning "mankind," "people," "men."

Fresh Fruit. References to fruit are notably lacking among ethnic dietary stereotypes, but a few occur. For example, Hawaiian women were once called *pineapple*. The English are still called *limey*. *Lime juicer* (or just *lime juice*) was used in the United States since the 1800s and the more familiar *limey* since about 1910. American and Australian servicemen in two world wars picked up and popularized the epithet for the English. Originally, the term was applied only to British sailors. *Limey* derives from the late eighteenth-century practice in the British Navy of serving lime juice to sailors on sea duty as a dietary supplement of Vitamin C to prevent scurvy. The variants *lemon eater* and *lemon sucker* are certainly a result of recent puckery toward the English.

Liquor, Wine, Beer, and Soda. You are what you eat—and drink. *Whiskey mick* is a slur on an Irishman. British Canadians were named *bing boy*, which I speculate is a variant of *bingo boy*, a drunk. Englishmen were called *corkney*, which is a double pun on *Cockney* and *cork*, alluding to supposed Cockney drinking habits. Native Americans were by 1899 nicknamed *hooch* or *hootch*, inspired by their reputation for high alcohol consumption. *Hooch*, meaning liquor, is short for *Hoochinoo*, an alteration of *Hutsnuwu*, the name of an Alaskan Indian group who made liquor. In Boston about 1810–20, blacks called whites *ball face*. I speculate it is from "ball face" or "bald face," the name of a whiskey in the same period. Germans, probably only in this century, were sometimes called *hop head*, not from dope but from the hops in German beer.

Italians were dubbed *grape stomper* and earlier *wino*. Lee Pederson (1964) said *wino* was used in Chicago and alluded to the use of table wine. But I note that *wino* was listed by Weseen (1934) as a term for grape pickers, winery workers, and wine makers in California, many of whom were Italians. Also subject to the sin tax is *snuff dipper*, an old black term for white Southerners; many blacks and whites thought snuff dipping was a filthy, loathsome habit. The only soft drink that has become an ethnic slur is *Pepsi*, a popular nickname for French Canadians, referring to their alleged predilection for Pepsi Cola.

Nuts. The humble peanut or goober pea is the only nut-like food whose name became an ethnic slur. Blacks were derided with *peanut*, not only because they ate them (a custom of white *and* black Southerners), but also because *peanut* is slang for a person or anything of small value. White Southerners, especially residents of the peanut-growing states, beginning in the nineteenth century, were called *goober grabber*. *Goober* is from African Kimbundu *nguba*, a type of peanut, and is a genuine Africanism. Assuming that all food vendors nibble on their goods from time to time, I will add that Italians were called *chestnut stabbers*, from the stereotype of immigrant street vendors selling roasted chestnuts. (Similarly, Italians were also called *banana peddlars* and *banana pushers*, from the old association with fruit vending.)

Dessert. As far as sweets are concerned, I found only one, and it stretches the point. In Chinese-American restaurants, after a meal, one gets a saucer with the check and a *fortune-cookie*, actually an American invention and much later a punning nickname for an attractive young Chinese woman.

SLURS FROM ACTIVITIES ASSOCIATED WITH FOOD

Harvesting food has given us *mushroom picker* for Czechs, from the popular pastime of foraging in Central Europe, and *chili picker* for Mexicans. Methods of cooking served *boiled dinner* to the Irish, *chow* to the Chinese from Cantonese *cha'ao* (fry), and *frito* to Mexicans from Spanish *frito*, fried, and a dish of fried food. *Frito* was surely reinforced by the former "Frito Bandito" corn chip commercials, which portrayed an offensive cartoon of a Mexican maven of the munchies. Even a manner of eating may be reflected in the name *chew* or *chaw* for an Irishman; the apparently related name *chew mouth* was perhaps for the noisy table manners of immigrant Irish working men. In the black street slang of Los Angeles, the Chinese and other Asian groups are called *chop sticks*. An allusion to the religiously prescribed preparation of food is in the name *kosher cutie* for a Jewish girl or woman.

DIETS OF DESTITUTION

Actual starvation among the poor whites in the South was common in the nineteenth century and even later. The practice of geophagy, seeking some nourishment from eating earth or clay, writes folklorist Francis W. Bradley (1964), gave the names *sandlapper* and *clay eater* to poor whites.[2] Southern blacks also called poor whites *clay eater*, as well as *hay eater*, which may allude to an animal. Blacks also called poor whites *rosin chewer*, from an apparent practice of chewing if not eating pine rosin. The emaciated physical appearance of poor whites led blacks to name them *thin people*.

Russians in this country were sometimes called *candle eater*, whose allusion eludes me, unless it refers to events in Europe and actually eating candle tallow, perhaps in an attempt to avert starvation. *Hungry* for Hungarian may be just a pun on *Hungary*, though it may also allude to the appetites of workingmen.

THE SERVING OF DIETARY SLURS

Food slurs are often formed by using the food referent as an adjective to modify *-head*, *-eater*, *-belly*, and other words. This device derogates the very activity of eating ethnic food, as well as the group who eats it. Rude table manners are imputed by the nouns *-snapper*, *-gobbler*, *-chomper*, *-guzzler*, *-sucker*, and *-grabber*. The manner of raising food to the mouth is derided in *spaghetti bender* and *taco bender*. The noun *-eater*, "one who eats," and rarely *-chewer* and *-swallower*, occur most often (fifteen items). After one has eaten, the food is in the *-belly* or *-gut* (five items), and the stomach so laden stands for the ethnic person. After one has eaten enough of these things, the logic of ethnic slurring seems to suggest, one becomes a *cabbage head*, a *potato head*, a *spaghetti head*, and others. The head, being the seat of personality, makes equating a person's head with what one eats a profound slur.

GREASER AND *GREASEBALL*

All this is a useful context to look at the old question of whether *greaser* or *greaseball*, which have been applied to a variety of Mediterranean and Latin American groups, refer to the heavy use of oil and fat in cooking or to the popular stereotype of an "oily" or "greasy" physical appearance. My sources show that *greaseball* has been applied to Greeks, Italians, and Puerto Ricans. *Greaser* was used for Italians, Puerto Ricans, and as early as 1836 for Mexicans. Mexicans were also called *grease gut*, *grease boy*, and *oiler*. Long ago a few amateur etymologists suggested that the names *greaser* and *oiler* for Mexicans came from the occupation of lubricating the wheels of railway cars, but that is fantastic folk etymology. A dual influence of the two stereotypes of generous amounts of fat in cooking and swarthy appearance probably account for *greaser* and *greaseball*. Mexican country cooking is notably fatty but Southern Italian cooking is not. *Greaser* recently emerged as an urban class epithet, a seeming counterpart to the (originally Southern) rural class epithet *redneck*.

All these slurs in American slang indicate a great historical awareness of alien ethnic food, its preparation, and the eating of it—another case of dislike for the unlike. Most of the dietary stereotypes have to do with simple, staple, but distinctive foods associated with immigrants and other low-status groups. Ethnic name-calling traffics at one level in highly visible cultural differences. But more basic than culture clash, hurling epithets has to do with putting ethnic persons and groups into their place and serves a primordial need to establish a pecking order in the plural community and society.

NOTES

1. Redall in 1889 reported that *beefheads* was a nickname for Texans. Some think residents of that state constitute an ethnic group. The allusion is certainly to the beef industry and the prominence of beef in the Texan diet.

2. *New York Times* (February 13, 1984) reported that the practice of geophagy persists in the American South to this day, though it is waning.

CHAPTER 6

FLIPPITY FLOPPITY: THE SEMANTIC INVERSION AND TRANSMIGRATION OF SLURS

ANYONE WHO MUSES on the surprisingly subtle semantics of the informal and usually offensive names for ethnic groups is struck by how their meanings vary according to the social context in which they are used. Meanings change, sometimes radically, depending on the speaker, the hearer, the relation between them, and even on who is overhearing them. Ethnic labels also change with the times, or flip, from negative slurs to positive names. Less well appreciated is the fact that some slurs, keeping their offensiveness, detach from one target group, transmigrate, or hippity hop, and attach to another group. The word histories of a few names go through even more complicated gyrations.

The most striking, but simplest instances of semantic inversion have been when oppressed groups, notably blacks in this country, took infamous slurs and turned them into symbols of unification and ethnic pride. Long ago African Americans turned the hated word *nigger*, especially its nadir *ba–ad nigger*, into ironic terms of admiration. Folklorist Alan Dundes, tracing the semantic change of *ba–ad nigger* (in a comment in Brearley 1973), describes the subtle and rich process by which the antebellum *ba–ad nigger*, a black who in whites' eyes represented the lowest, meanest sort, was turned around in black ethnic culture to signify a role of rebelliousness, bravado, and testiness toward whites. Dundes concludes: "Here then we may have a remarkable folk transformation of an outgroup's intended term of opprobrium into a positive compliment as understood by members of the in-group." In the late 1960s, the name *blacks* for African Americans, formerly a derogatory label used by whites, was inverted and is now the preferred, but perhaps passing, name for the group, and this is discussed further in the next chapter.

Following the same rule, names for certain low-status white groups have been semantically inverted by their targets. *Coonass* for a Louisiana Acadian has been cheerfully adopted by the target group and may be seen printed on tee shirts. *Redneck* derived from the appearance of a Southern farm laborer who got a red, sun-burned neck from working in the fields. When shirtless, the sight of his red neck was thought to resemble the marking of a male red-headed woodpecker, or "peckerwood" inverted in the folk way. The term *redneck* was later applied to any working-class Southerner in the genteel view. (*Peckerwood*, in the related sense, became a black term for whites.) Presidential candidate George Wallace of Alabama was the force that helped turn *redneck* into an honorific in white, working-class Southern society. Similarly, *hillbilly* for a Southern highlander is now even the preferred self-descriptive in self-conscious circles. Today these labels, often as not, are worn proudly, if defensively, and often with great humor.

The inversion strips the name of harm, and some bearers seem to try to live up the challenge of the stereotype. On the other hand, white majorities, especially when they are confident and secure in their position (and so sometimes a little guilty about it, too), ironically call themselves *gringos*, *anglos*, and *WASPs* to express a certain, uneasy relation to the minorities who gave them those names in the first place.

When minorities use these epithets today, they can point to the fact that their majority targets have acquiesced to the label and, so, can insist slyly that no offense is intended.

In another sort of semantic inversion, some group epithets start as ingroup names of no derogation and become outgroup terms of great pejoration. The name *Canuck* was not traditionally considered derogatory by either Francophones or Anglophones in Canada, though it may have later become so in the knowledge of how the term was used in the United States. Note the name of the Vancouver Canucks, a famous hockey team. In popular culture, the name also became a symbol of Canada, in the personification of Johnny Canuck, much like John Bull for England and Uncle Sam for the United States. One no less than Prime Minister Pierre Elliott Trudeau in 1977 said he had never heard the name used pejoratively in Canada. But Quebeckers in the United States consider *canuck* highly offensive, about the worst name they can be called. Anglophone Canadians and Americans around the border of the New England states and Quebec probably applied the name *canuck* to the lower-status, French-speaking Acadians. The name, while not necessarily offensive in Canada, was nonetheless offensive to Francophone immigrants who felt marginal in New England. In the 1972 Presidential primaries, a rumor was circulated that Maine's Senator Edmund Muskie, who is of Polish background, had referred to U. S. Quebeckers as "canucks"—and that is a fighting word in Maine. The dirty trick brought Muskie temporary embarassment and required strong denials.

Other ingroup terms in a similar way became outgroup epithets. *Cracker* is a positive or at least a humorous self-label for many Georgians. But in and beyond Georgia it was and remains a class epithet, and it is more recently a black term for any white, Southerner or Northerner, who is thought to be a racist. *Peckerwood*, the folk inversion of *woodpecker*,

was for many years a Southernerism of no particular con-
tempt for a white rustic. Blacks eventually turned the term
on whites in general as a name of great derision.

The infamous epithet *wop* for an Italian derives from the
Neapolitan and Sicilian *guappo*: a handsome, daring, and
strong man—a dude. Anthony Burgess, the British novelist
and polyglot, reports that to this day Neapolitans call themselves the *guapi*—the pretty ones. Abraham Roback reported second hand (from his Italian barber) that a short
form, *uap*, was used in the local speech of Palazza, between
Bari and Calabria. Several scholars have speculated that
guappo, or possibly a short form, in the 1880s and later in
this country was used among immigrant men from southern
Italy as a friendly greeting. The slur, now phonetically spelled
wop, may have begun as a mock of this overheard word.
Ethnic epithets sometimes begin as a mimicking of emblem-
atic words, phrases, or speech sounds of another language
community.

A few ethnic slurs have detached from their original referents, transmigrated, and attached to another national group.
Italian Americans, historically a much-slurred ethnicity, have
been the targets of two transmigrating slurs—*dago* and *guinea*.
Dago is an Americanism and an alteration of the Spanish and
Portuguese personal name *Diego*, James. Since the early
eighteenth century the name was used for Spaniards and,
later, for Mexicans, though today rarely for either. About
1880 *dago* detached from Spanish-speaking groups, hopped
over, and attached to Italians, soon exclusively. *Guinea* originally was an old, antebellum term for blacks. It started as a
slaver's term for black men who were forced to immigrate
from the Guinea Coast of Africa. The reapplication of *guinea*
to Italians after 1880 and the New Immigration, in which
Southern Italians were so prominent, said in effect that the
greenhorns were no better than blacks.

While the Italians gained two new slurs in this manner,
they also lost one in exactly the same way and at about the

same time. *Spic, spik,* or *spick,* a slur that refers to almost any low-status Latin American, but especially to Mexicans and Puerto Ricans, was perhaps originally a term for Italians. The origin is traditionally assumed to be a mocking of an accented pronunciation of "(No) *speak the* (English)," comically rendered as *spicka* or *spiggoty.* But Stuart Berg Flexner in *I Hear America Talking* wrote that *spic* "may have come from the expression 'no spicka Engleesh,' but the word was originally *spig* and may have come from *spaghetti,* since until 1915 *spig* was used to refer to an Italian" (1976, 322). Still earlier, in the *Dictionary of American Slang* (1975), Flexner said that *spic* or *spig* was "shortened from 'spaghetti,' reinforced by the traditional phrase 'No spicka da English.' " I will add that an Italian was also called a *spaghetti* and its short form *spag. Spiggoty* sounds very much like a version of *spaghetti* and *spig* a thinning of *spag,* and who knows with all these new names for pastas. In the historical lexicon of all ethnic slurs, phonetic mocking is rare but dietary ridicule is common. I speculate that early in this century *spiggoty,* drawn thin from *spaghetti,* trimmed to bite-size as *spig,* al dente as *spic,* dropped from Italians and hopped, no flopped, over to the plate of Latin Americans.

Other ethnic labels have histories of even more turns of meaning. First, let me return briefly to *canuck.* The name, in its early history, might have been borrowed from the speech of an early Canadian minority as an informal name for that group. Later it somehow emerged as a national symbol of all Canadians, and yet later, in its unfavorable sense, settled upon Francophone Canadians in the United States. W. W. Schuhmacher's hypothesis (1989) that *canuck* derives from a blend of the *can* of *Canadian* and the *nuk* of the Inuit or Eskimo word *inuk* for 'man' or 'Eskimo,' would support such a word history. Mitford Mathews (1975), on the other hand, argued that *canuck* derives from *kanacka,* Hawaiian for "man," which was borrowed from and used for indentured Sandwich Islanders who served as canoemen in colonial Canada. The spelling of the first syllables of *Canadian* and *canuck* at any rate accounts for the popular etymology that *canuck* came from *Canada* and *Canadian*.

Chicano and, lately, *Chicana*, a truncated, regional pronunciation of *Mexicano*, apparently emerged and was used for perhaps fifty years as an ingroup label among border-area Mexicans for those subgroups among them who identified more with traditional culture than with the more modern Tex-Mex culture. *Chicano* apparently began as a mild status pejorative among Mexican Americans before it was borrowed by outsiders and used as a slur for all Mexicans who lived in the *barrios*. Around 1968 politically conscious young Mexican Americans reappropriated the term and made it an expression of ethnic pride. But the name is still resisted by older, politically more cautious Mexican Americans. A survey in 1979 showed that only ten percent of Americans of Mexican descent preferred the new name (Torres, 1983). *Chicano* is still used perjoratively by some Anglophone Americans, and in the Northeast it is sometimes ignorantly and contemptuously applied to Puerto Ricans.

In other instances, like pissing into the wind, offensive names have blown back onto the groups that originated them. *Honky*, the black generic for whites, is simply a borrowing—and pronounced in black English—of the originally white epithet *hunky* for an immigrant, central European laborer. Since early in this century blacks had heard the term *hunky* become almost generic for a white, roughneck laborer—a redneck, and so blacks just generalized it further to all whites. Blacks in 1960s street vernacular also borrowed from the white majority another of their slurs for a white minority and turned it on all whites. The name *paddy* for any white person and a seemingly unmanly *patty* are simply blow-backs of the old derogatory term for the Irish, *paddy*. A variant but more ephemeral black term for a white was *dap*, backslang for *pad*, a shortening of *paddy*.

This chapter concludes the discussion of the old fighting words in historical American speech. By tracing their histories and analyzing how they work in social and cultural contexts, I have tried to defuse and neutralize the horrific effect of the words themselves. Unfortunately, some of the old fighting words are still heard in American life, even lately on college campuses, and we all need to think a great deal more about the problematic ethnic relations that give rise to offensive speech. We now turn to a somewhat newer and "higher" order of ethnic slurring that has grown in importance, especially since the end of the Second World War— a variety of more "subtle" devices that have been more tolerated in contemporary society but that echo the same sentiments as the old fighting words.

Part II

Newer Devices

Since the world is so full of a number of things, as Robert Louis Stevenson said, we must categorize and simplify in order to comprehend. But the reduction of complexity entails a great danger, since the line between enlightening epitome and vulgarized distortion is so fine.

—Stephen Jay Gould, in a book review, 1984

CHAPTER 7

SLY SLURS: MISPRONUNCIATION AND DECAPITALIZATION OF GROUP NAMES

DEROGATORY, GENERIC NAMES for ethnic groups in historical American English, or in the language of any plural society, serve social uses of informal social control in the speech community similar to those that personal nicknames serve in smaller groups. Most nicknames for outgroups attempt to stratify groups in the local community, or to protest the ranking, by replacing the proper, preferred name of a group with an altogether different name with negative semantics. But sometimes name-callers grudgingly concede the accepted, standard name for a group, including its spelling, and then deliberately alter the conventional or polite pronunciation of the name. The slur is connoted by denying the standard of the target's speech community. Printed representations of these phonetic alterations usually appear later, which conventionalizes the slur, print reinforcing speech and the converse. A second, slyer technique of pejoration gives lip service to the preferred, proper name of the group in speech and in spelling, but in writing denies the conventional capital initial to the group name in order to connote the slur.

Both devices are, of course, well known, but are of additional interest because they reveal a complicated interplay of ethnic ideology and the usage of names for ethnically stigmatized groups. Taken together these and similar devices display a microcosm of ethnic discourse in American life.

PHONETIC ALTERATIONS

Deliberate mispronunciation is the more common of the two techniques. The same tactic of verbal abuse is applied at the individual level to ethnically stigmatized personal names and at the group level to ethnic group names. Linguist John M. Lipski explains how prejudice is expressed in deliberate mispronunciations of "foreign" surnames, and how the incidence of this varies with the level of prejudice in local communities. Prejudice also prompts the mispronunciation of names of nationalities and of ethnic groups, and best known are *Negro*, *Italian*, and *Arab*. Phonetic twists however can be put on the name of any ethnic group with the same pejorative effect.

The dialectologists Raven I. McDavid (1960) and Leas (1981) have treated the white Southern regional pronunciations of *Negro* as *NIG-rah* and other variants, which came to symbolize the undercurrent of racial tensions in the South. Educated African Americans, especially in the North, and especially after the Second World War, sought to establish *NEE-gro* as the polite form. McDavid and Leas however show that *NIG-rah* and other variants are, in fact, the polite forms in dialects and that they were not usually intended to slur or to connote the hated cognate. Yet when whites, as the dominant group, finally understood that blacks preferred *NEE-gro*, but persisted in using traditional pronunciations, though faultlessly spelling them *Negro*, the resistance to change in this small matter was at least provocative and sometimes nothing more than thinly disguised hostility (Lipski, 114).

Lipski also discusses the deliberate mispronunciation of *Arab*, a popular generic name for various Arab or Arabic American national groups. The pronunciation *AY-rab* is still heard among older, less educated Americans, perhaps only because, Lipski suggests, it recalls the long *a* of *Arabia*. But people who know better sometimes deliberately say *AY-rab* as a slur, and Americans of Arabic background generally find it offensive.

The pronunciation of *Italian* as *EYE-talian* is also dialect, but has been abused in a similar way. The phonetically-spelled print rendering, *Eyetalian* is old, dating at least to 1840, and was probably intended to mock the dialectal pronunciation. Today, the pronunciation is often taken as a slur, and the spelling always is. This pronunciation also suggests to some the old slur *eyetie*, which was also popular during the First World War. To some persons not in the Southern speech community, the regional pronunciations of *Italian* may sound like a deliberate slur. The South and its speechways irrationally linger in the minds of some Americans as a singular locus of cultural bigotry and its expression. Jimmy Carter, during his first presidential campaign in 1976, was pressed to apologize publicly for pronouncing *Italian* as *EYE-talian*. The sounds came out of Carter's mouth naturally and without malice. Up north, Carter learned, *EYE-talian* is a fighting word, almost on a level with *wop*. This pronunciation and the variant *eye-TILE-ians* were common in old urban vaudeville routines, which abounded in gross ethnic and other social stereotypes, humor, and derisive nicknames—and memories of cultural abuse are long.

DENIAL OF CAPITAL INITIALS

In standard English usage, the proper names of national and religious groups are written with a capital initial. The rule is occasionally taken as an honorific gesture that can be bestowed or denied at the pleasure of the writer or editor.

To deny a capital letter to the name of an ethnic group symbolically diminishes the social status of the group in the speech community by the word magic of diminishing the initial letter. To deny, say, *Jew* the capital initial is clearly a slur and the device has been used in the hate literature. The user concedes the pronunciation and the spelling, but in print the dignity of the name is taken away. The business of denying a disliked ethnic group a big letter also occurs in other language communities with this convention of capitalization. Before the Second World War, for example, certain Polish writers refused to capitalize the initial of *Niemiec*, the Polish name for "German" (Roback 1944, 268).[1]

The most famous case of non-capitalization in American English is certainly that of *Negro*. The name began its centuries-long career with a lower-case initial but after Reconstruction aspired to a capital initial. In the decades around 1900, *colored* competed with *negro* for the preferred, proper name for the group. A residue of this usage is prominent today in the name of the National Association for the Advancement of Colored People, (NAACP), which was founded in 1910. *Afro-American*, first recorded in 1853, was seriously proposed in 1880, but it was not taken up, and it was to be eighty years or more before it was to gain a measure of use. Finally, *negro* emerged as the proper name preferred by many blacks and by white liberals. Settling on the name was not to be the end of it. Soon, a campaign began for capitalizing the initial, and the debate turned on ideology as much as anything. A side debate was over whether *negro* was a relative color descriptive, like *fair*, *dark*, or for that matter *black* and *white*, and hence had no claim on capitalization. Or was *negro*, in effect, a national name, like Englishman, German, or Spaniard, or a group name, like *Jew*, and so should be capitalized?

H. L. Mencken (1963, 379–82) recounts, not wholly approving, how black leaders and the black press urged the capitalization of *Negro* as a recognition of the dignity of black people and of their equality with other groups. Mencken cites the "irreverent" black columnist George Schuyler, who argued in the 1930s and 1940s that capitalization would, in effect, harden the stereotype of black people. Schuyler thought *negro* was a descriptive, not a group denomination. Nonetheless, the *New York Times* had in 1930 announced that it would capitalize *Negro*. Federal government publications followed in 1933. Other publications, depending on how liberal their inclinations, followed. Most of the nation's press had complied by the late 1940s. A few small Southern newspapers defiantly kept the lower-case initial well into the 1950s. The beginning of the Civil Rights Movements effectively marked an end to this petty dispute.

A few decades after this battle had been won, history repeated itself with a similar technical controversy about the capitalization of *black*. But new ideologies confounded the issue. After 1968 the name *Negro* quickly fell from favor among younger black people. For decades some politically-minded blacks had objected to the word *Negro*—with or without the capital initial—because of its associations with slavery and because it was an alien name of Spanish and Portuguese origin foisted upon blacks by whites. The emergence of the black pride movement and the militant and separatist turn of the Civil Rights Movement prompted a change of names in keeping with the new identity; it was to be *black*. The capitalization, or not, of *black* and, this time, too, of *white*, became once again a complicated game of ethnic discourse in miniature.

It did not seem to matter that *black* was one of the oldest names used by the slavers and that it was, often as not, used as an epithet down to the 1960s. Blacks recognized that they—blacks—and whites were, more than anything else, political camps, and the word *black* represented a one-to-one opposition to *white*. The names—each has one syllable and five letters—were polar opposites, and each word is laden with historical, even mystical symbolism. The white press and academic writers did not know how to respond, though some tried to follow the erratic lead of new, unsettled, still-emerging black usages. Earlier in the 1960s some had eagerly adopted *Afro-American*, then still less than common. Yet the U. S. Bureau of the Census in the count of 1970 offered black citizens the choice of identifying themselves as "Negro," "Afro-American," or "Black." *Black* was soon accepted by the national press. The *New York Times* rode out the transition by alternating *black* and *Negro*, sometimes using *black* as an adjective but keeping *Negro* as a noun. Soon *black* came into general use and *Negro* was out. Now it was *black* and *white*—neat, simple, and symmetrical.

The lower-case initial in *black* and *white* also seemed to take account of the idea that blacks and whites were not ethnic monoliths or "nationalities," as much as traditionally estranged entities of some other sort. Then the old question of capitalization arose again, but with some new issues. Some academic writers and journalists, probably recalling the struggle to capitalize *Negro*, rushed to capitalize *black*, both as an adjective and as a noun. But this vanguard seemed to miss the political point of the forthrightness offered by an all lower-case *black*. Ironically, capitalizing the new name could detract from the new political idea it represented and make *Black* in this particular only a replacement for the rejected *Negro* and with no change of meaning. These writers and editors seemed to fear that the all lower-case *black* might be taken as mildly pejorative, like its pre-1930s predecessor *negro*. Or perhaps the capitalized *Black* was an effort to set the new name apart from the old *black*, a historical epithet.

At any rate many writers and editors in the late 1960s began using the capitalized *Black*, both as noun and adjective, while keeping the conventional lower-case *white*. This, to be sure, destroyed the symmetry of the two ideas. Did this, they must have wondered, make *Black* with a capital initial look like a sop? Or, from another perspective, did a big *B* towering over a little *w* hint of confrontation and "demands"? Some users settled down with the asymmetrical forms *B*lack and *w*hite, but never the reverse. Some took no chances and capitalized both, while others kept the lower-case initial for both. After two decades writers and editors have not yet arrived at consensus. Mostly, I see the symmetrical *black* and *white* used in what I read. Nonetheless, some journalists, academic writers, and editors who seem eager to display their sensitivity to racial matters use the upper-case *B*lack and the lower-case *w*hite.

Prescription may have a certain logic and historical sense, but usage, for better or worse, will eventually carry the day. Yet popular and prevailing usages, as surely as imposed elite usages, reflect ideology—the manipulation of ideas and symbols for political goals. Whether both names are capitalized or not is a trivial matter, but capitalizing one name and not the other is a political gesture—ideology in typography. But at this level it is not always cogent. Capitalizing only *Black* can smack of indulgence when done by white writers and of, well, "signifying" when done by black writers.

It could be argued that both names are, or have become, proper nouns and so should be capitalized. On the other hand, can we not hope that black and white are, or should be, informal, temporary matters and that their opposition ought not be hardened symbolically with capital letters any more than it is? South African English usage, I gather from afar, seems to favor *Black* and *White*—both capitalized; in that social and political context it makes more sense to connote intractable relations. But in the American context the simplicity and symmetry of *b*lack and *w*hite avoids casting the names—symbolically opponents—into emblems.

But the whole issue of capitalization—and the discourse it symbolizes—may soon be turned aside if the noun and adjective *African-American* is successfully introduced. The Rev. Jesse Jackson recently suggested that it is now time for American blacks to take the more fruitful identity and name of *African Americans*, to take their place alongside other

American ethnic groups whose names refer to "some land base, some historical cultural base." The use of *African American* already seems to be gaining ground and it has been used alternately with *black* throughout this book. The wide adoption of the new label would please many social scientists, for it would connote ethnicity over color and connote equality in pluralism.

Noncapitalization signifies the historical weakness of a minority group; the struggle for capitalization signifies the rising status of a historically oppressed group; and decapitalization has sometimes signified efforts to repress competing groups. We can also expect to see the final permutation: decapitalization to signify the declining status of a formerly dominant group. The so-called WASPs, whose new name comes from the wonderfully pronounceable acronym for White Anglo-Saxon Protestant(s), were high in the popular consciousness in the 1960s and 1970s. The coincidence of a group that both is in decline and has an acronym for a name offers an unusual opportunity for ethnic conflict to result in multiple and progressive decapitalization.

As the acronym *WASP* became widely used and became a meaningful sound as much as a spelled word, its original and acronymic meaning became hazy and half-forgotten.[2] An acronym is customarily spelled, at least at first, with all capital letters—*WASP*. But acronyms tend to slide first into a capitalized initial and finally into all lower case, like the descent from *RADAR*, to *Radar*, down to *radar*. Some journalists and editors wearied of the pretense that the epithet *WASP* was merely a denotative, neutral acronym and began to use *Wasp*. The *American Heritage Dictionary* in 1970 gave authority to this by listing *Wasp*, *WASP*, and *wasp*, in that order, which suggests that the all upper-case form was beginning to lose its grip. A few writers mischievously flirted with the all lower-case *wasp*, making it into a common noun and by connotation a pejorative. But recently I have seen here and there a rehabilitation to a proper acronymic, all upper-case *WASP*, perhaps indicating an awareness of the pejorative suggestion in decapitalization and attempting to set a distance between the two meanings.

A SINGULAR PUNCH

Yet a third, slyer technique of connotative slurring has been heard by those with their ears tuned to nuance in usage. Do the proper nouns *Jew*, *Swede*, and *Pole* have a slightly pejorative connotation when used in the singular, but not when used in the plural? I have noticed some writers and speakers, for example, shying away from the singular *Jew* and instead using the phrase *Jewish person*. Even the plural *Jews* seems to be used more and more to refer to the Jewish community—the Jewry—such as *American Jews*, but not to a smaller, informal group of Jews, who are more likely to be called *Jewish persons* or *Jewish people*. I have also noticed a similar preference for *Swedish* over *Swede* and *Polish* over *Pole*. But I do not hear a parallel preference for *Finnish* over *Finn* or *Danish* over *Dane*. What's the difference?

I think the old, various derogatory uses of *Jew*, *Pole*, and *Swede* have tainted these perfectly good proper names. The unabridged dictionaries record the several secondary and derogatory meanings of *Jew*, one of which is for any person who drives a hard bargain. Linguist Sharon Henderson Taylor (1974) has written of how *Pole* and *Swede* have been used as generic terms for any stupid person, regardless of their ethnicity. These proper names have also been used in compound forms: *dumb Pole*, *dumb Swede*, *big Swede*, and *dirty Jew*. Even without the derogatory adjectives, the sensitive ear is conditioned to complete the phrase. Also, the singular *Jew* has been used attributively and ungrammatically in derogatory compounds such as *Jew boy* and *Jew store* and in verb forms as *to jew* and *to jew down*.

To some, *Jew* has a patent, even a harsh sound, which

seems somehow softened by the adjectival *Jewish*. Perhaps *Jew* sounds too "ethnic," whereas *Jewish* sounds more "assimilated." At any rate, *Jewish person* is now considered more polite than *Jew*. Dr. Jonathan Miller, the English physician, comedian, author, and theatrical director, reportedly mocked this when he was referred to as a *Jew*: "I'm not a Jew, just Jew-*ish*—not the whole hog."

NOTES

1. Etymologically and historically, noncapitalization is the least of the slur in *Niemiec*. In Polish and in Russian, the word for "German" is related to the word for one who is mute or dumb— *niemy* in Polish. In the early history of the region, the Slavic-speaking people regarded their Germanic-speaking neighbors to the west as barbarians whose language was incomprehensible and, so, figuratively they were mute or dumb.

2. William Safire in his political column in the *New York Times* more than once has felt it necessary, despite the redundancy of the idea of "white" already in the term (white *and* Anglo-Saxon), to remind his readers that *WASPs* are white. Describing the fiasco of a United Nations vote near the end of the Carter administration, Safire (March 6, 1980) wrote that Cyrus Vance was "white, Wasp . . ." and several years later on August 23, 1984, he referred to "white WASP women." This also confirms my more general suspicion that *WASP* has become a euphemism, or perhaps a dysphemism, for Protestants. Also see Chapter 10.

CHAPTER 8

SLY SLURS: EUPHEMISMS AND CODEWORDS

SLY SLURS ALSO appear as codewords and euphemisms. A codeword is usually an innocent-sounding term substituted for an unacceptable term, such as a slur, and the motive is usually mischief. Good, though naive intentions, on the other hand, usually lie behind euphemisms. A euphemism is a word that is used to avoid another word thought to be too direct, blunt, harsh, or offensive. Hugh Rawson in *A Dictionary of Euphemisms & Other Doubletalk* (1981) tells how terms such as *culturally deprived, underprivileged, disadvantaged, minority group*, and *minority*, and even the word *poor*, are euphemisms for poor black and Spanish-speaking Americans.

The good people in the so-called helping professions are justly satirized for the euphemisms they coin and use for impoverished segments of ethnic groups. Most such euphemisms and codewords are or eventually become thinly disguised allusions to those several groups who are disproportionately among the lowest-income segments of the population.

The Second Barnhart Dictionary of New English (1980) points out that "a paradoxical feature of euphemisms is that when the character or meaning of what they describe catches up with the euphemism itself they lose their character as substitutes and come to denote the very same unpleasant fact or reality they were meant to disguise." Terms such as *urban poor* and *culturally deprived* started out as euphemisms to denote the most impoverished among black and Spanish-speaking Americans. As the words spread into popular speech, people began to associate the reality of the ethnic and class referents more closely with the euphemism and the words lost their euphemistic ability. The euphemisms are then generally understood to refer precisely to the ethnic and class reality they were meant to cloak.

A further paradox enters when these former euphemisms fall into the hands of sly name-callers and become genteel codewords for blacks and other groups. African Americans complained in the 1960s that the euphemism *culturally deprived* had become a slur on black history and culture. Blacks also rightfully began to resent the implicit pejoration of the term *nonwhite*. A variety of other terms are still enjoying a respectable life of euphemism, but I think they will soon fall into being codewords. Evasive language can serve the evasive purposes of both good and bad intentions.

POVERTY SPEAK

Certain journalists and writers, like Edwin Newman, delight in laying at the feet of social scientists—anthropologists, economists, political scientists, sociologists—responsibility for the pretentious jargon, unnecessary neologisms, and euphemisms that we see used to discuss social problems. Actually, most of the obscurantist jargon and euphemisms come from welfare workers, public school administrators, family problem counselors, government bureaucrats, and people in the helping professions. It is mostly a language of "social concern" used by those whose job it is to manage the poor and to justify policies on the problem of the poor.

William Morris and Mary Morris, the well-known lexicographers and authors of a syndicated column on language, tell a story related to them in a letter from a woman complaining of the semantic hocus-pocus of the aptly named "poverty industry:" "I used to think I was poor," she wrote. "Then they told me I wasn't poor; I was *needy*. Then they said it was self-defeating to think of myself as needy, that I was *culturally deprived*. Then they told me deprived was a bad image, that I was *underprivileged*. Then they told me that *underprivileged* was overused, that I was *disadvantaged*. I still don't have a dime—but I have a great vocabulary!" (1975, 257).

Another group of euphemistic terms for the poor of ethnic minorities is given life by the historical ambivalence most Americans feel toward their cities. The adjective *urban* has become an epithet in American English and is being used as a euphemism for lower-class African-American and Latin-American cultures. Our intellectual history of anti-urbanism has long led us to associate cities with social problems—an attitude that tragically became a self-fulfilling prophecy when so many middle-class whites fled the cities. We not only think of the cities as the locus of social problems but also have come to believe the fiction that cities somehow cause social problems. City life, it is widely believed, is not fit for human consumption.

The poor of several ethnic minorities are disproportionately concentrated in the centers of our cities. The flight of the middle classes of all groups to the suburbs is one of the main reasons for the isolation of the poor of all groups in the cities. The association of poverty and particularly blacks with the cities is the thinking behind such phrases as *inner-city youth*, *urban youth*, and *urban poor*. These terms do not refer chiefly to the urban character of the poor but refer to their class and ethnic character. These phrases avoid the directness of uttering such phrases as "young black people" or "poor Puerto Ricans." "Urban" is now widely understood to pertain to ethnic minorities and their problems. *Suburban,* on the other hand, signals white, middle-class things—good and wholesome things. The epithet *urban* also slyly suggests an "explanation" of their poverty and community problems, so as to disassociate responsibility for the problem from the suburbs and the rest of the country.

NONWHITE IS UNWHITE

In an area as emotionally sensitive as ethnicity, groups and individuals of those groups ought to be called any ethnic-group name they wish to be called and the name ought to be pronounced and written in any way they like. We more generally and faithfully accord this consideration to the personal names of individuals, and ethnic identities are often just as close to people's self-esteem. The problem, of course, is that ethnic groups are not always of one mind on what they wish to be called. It is sometimes difficult for others to determine what ethnic label is acceptable to most and offensive to almost none. Ideally, perhaps we should have less need and fewer occasions to speak of ethnicity at all. But we are not yet fully comfortable with our diversity and may never be. The problem of ethnic labeling is especially acute in cases of emergent and recently identified ethnicities. Most troublesome are the grossly generic but straight-sounding labels that lump together diverse ethnic groups and make political rhetoric.

Nonwhite, a supposedly neutral term of jargon used by the U. S. Bureau of the Census, became used as a euphemism for blacks in the 1950s and 1960s. The Census Bureau formerly used *nonwhite* to label a residual category in its statistical reports when there are too few "nonwhite" persons to break them down group by group. *Nonwhite* is the catch-all category for the roughly 20 percent of the population that is black, Asian, or Native American.

Nonwhite was quickly seized for a term that could be used to refer to all racial minorities as racial minorities, cloaked in the respectability of U. S. Census terminology. The ethnic minorities who became the targets of this new usage rightly found the term offensive because it defines them as the negation of white and so something lesser. Our American term *nonwhite* parallels the British term *Colored* (with a capital *C*), which is used indiscriminately and often pejoratively for all dark-complexioned *Immigrants* (another British slur) and their children in the United Kingdom.

The term *nonwhite* soon passed into that foggy region between slang and jargon. In the early 1960s skittish white professors said *nonwhites* as a nice word for *Negroes*, before they were emboldened to use *blacks* by the spirit of the Civil Rights Movement. Spanish-speaking groups also were sometimes called *nonwhites* to acknowledge that they too were the objects of prejudice and discrimination. I recall one sociologist who wrote in the 1960s that Spanish-speaking groups ought to be called *nonwhites* for that was exactly the way prejudiced people regarded them.

Ethnics, Hispanics, Latinos, Chicanos, and *Appalachians*

An elementary principle of the relation of language to society is that new vocabulary is coined to express new awareness and new social concerns. In the 1960s and 1970s, five new proper names for ethnic groups came into the language. Each refers euphemistically to the working-class segments of various ethnic groups, that is, to ethnic persons who are not middle class. The terms reach for new meanings to denote new ethnic awareness and are formed from adjectives. Each of the new names has the eternal failing of euphemism; it is slipping into use as a codeword. Yet some are better than others.

Ethnics, the noun, is an intellectual's word that is little used by the "ethnics" themselves. The ethnics are the daughters, sons, and grandchildren of mostly Catholic immigrants from Eastern and Southern Europe, particularly Italians, Poles, and other Slavic groups. *Ethnics* had some limited use in the early 1940s by the sociologist W. Lloyd Warner in his famous "Yankee City" series of community studies to refer to low-status ethnic groups, including Jews, of recent immigration. *Ethnics* was revived and popularized to denominate those white groups who had a nostalgic upsurge of ethnic consciousness and pride in the late 1960s and early 1970s. Some think this pause in the assimilation of these groups was little more than a backlash against the supposed gains of blacks at a time when there was a seeming neglect of the problems of working-class white ethnic groups—the ethnics. *Ethnics* applies in practice only to the working-class segments of those groups, whose political expression and action is so often along ethnic lines. A few middle-class intellectuals of Eastern and Southern European background like to call themselves *ethnics*, but no one else would.

Until the early 1970s, with rare exception, *ethnic* was an adjective, not a noun, as any dictionary will confirm. Properly speaking, everyone is ethnic. But only certain groups are ethnics. Blacks and Jews are not ethnics, but are blacks and Jews. The Irish, though Catholic, and not ethnics because most are too assimilated and middle class. At any rate, I hear *ethnics*, born of euphemism, at worst slipping into a codeword for the most quarrelsome, least assimilated, white, mostly Catholic, city neighborhood groups who are inclined to defend their turf against integration. At best, it is becoming a mild epithet for working-class Catholics. Several college textbooks in the field of urban studies already have taken up *ethnics* as a euphemism for working-class Catholic groups.

In the 1970s, we gained an awareness of the new social reality that Spanish-speaking groups from Latin America had become the largest foreign-language community in the United States. Soon they are probably to become the largest class of minority groups, surpassing the size of the black population. Many of the new immigrants were poor and unskilled, and many of these newcomers were strikingly unassimilated. The new reality needed a new word. Bureaucrats, academics, and the press wanted a generic term specifically for the masses of unassimilated Latin Americans, so the name *Hispanics* was coined from the adjective *Hispanic* and soon was in wide use. *Latinos*, also straight from the adjectival combining form, competes, but is not heard as often as *Hispanics*.

All in all, *Latinos* may be the better term to denote the multi-ethnic reality of our immigrants from all Latin American nations and from all segments of their societies (Totti, 1987, 542). *Latinos* avoids some of the most proximate Eurocentric connotations of *Hispanics*, seems to refer more to a geographic than to a colonial cultural area, and seems to embrace a wider ethnic and racial reality. *Latinos* is increasingly preferred by the writers most sensitive to the ethnic issues and in time may come to compete seriously with the bureaucratic term *Hispanics*. Yet the standard English *Latin Americans* also catches these senses of *Latinos*, though neither all of its connotations nor its flavor of minority origin.

The word *Hispanic* until recently was an adjective, not a noun. But like *ethnics*, *Hispanics* became a noun to denote a certain segment of the people described by the adjective. *Hispanic*, the adjective, denotes all Latin Americans regardless of social class, for one of its dictionary meanings is "of or pertaining to Latin America or Latin Americans." But *Hispanics*, the noun, in usage more often than not, connotes the lower-income, less-assimilated persons of these groups. Middle-class persons of these groups are more likely to be thought of as "Mexican Americans," "Cuban Americans,"

"Colombian Americans," and so on, or aggregately as "Latin Americans." Another new term, *Hispanic Americans*, keeps the adjectival use of *Hispanic*. It seems to be a middle ground, avoiding some of the connotations of the noun *Hispanics*, but it is not often used.

Critics of the name *Hispanics* have argued that it indifferently categorizes and thereby effectively stereotypes some twenty million Americans from many different ethnic, racial, national, cultural, class, and religious backgrounds, who share little more than varieties of the Spanish language, and sometimes not even language. So-called "Hispanics" are mostly migrants to the United States from Mexico, Central America, and South America, and the Spanish-speaking areas of the Caribbean. The net of the label is sometimes thrown wider to include Portuguese-speaking Brazilians and even Europeans from Spain and Portugal who have settled in this country. Some Portuguese Americans, or Luso-Americans, reject the label of *Hispanics*. Occasionally, even French-speaking and English-speaking immigrants from Caribbean countries are loosely called *Hispanics*. Primary speakers of indigenous, South American Indian languages, are often lumped together with other "Hispanics" when they arrive in the United States.

In this coarse generic usage, the name *Hispanics* is questionably capitalized in writing, for it is not, strictly speaking, a proper noun and does not refer to a single entity of culture or national origin; and experimental and altogether respectful instances of the lower-case *hispanics* have been seen in print. *Asian* stands for the other large "racial" aggregate of this order but probably will not lose its capital initial. All refer to social constructions of "racial" categories. The name *Asian* encompasses immigrant peoples from the eastern part of the Asian continent and "Asian" regions of the Pacific basin. *Asian* arose in part as an avoidance of the older, Eurocentric term *Oriental*, which had become a pejorative, with or without the capital initial. The word *Asian* has always been conventionally capitalized and the historical weight of this usage will probably stay with the new ethnic meanings. *Asian* originally referred to the continent of Asia and *Hispanic* originally to the countries, peoples, and cultures of the Iberian peninsula. Both terms, more than either *black* or *white*, have a precedent for continuance of the traditional capitalization.

Hispanics and other terms of this ilk were introduced and promoted by people who found it bureaucratically or politically useful to denote large, diverse aggregates of ethnic peoples in a few simple categories. For some users these names signify the scandal of inequality in American society. For others the names serve to justify indifference to the diversity and humanity of the people they stand for. Like most euphemisms, codewords, and other avoidances, *Hispanics* also has taken on pejorative racial connotations in some parts of the country. It is not clear to me that *Hispanics* serves the upward social and economic mobility of its referents as much as it serves the political agenda of some of its users. The categorical referents would be most sensibly called *Latin Americans* and, whenever feasible, more particularly by the name of the country or commonwealth from which they migrated—such as *Mexican Americans*. The reason that such formations have not found wider favor is certainly because such names fail to connote inequality.

The usage of *Latin Americans* and the particulars of national and commonwealth names, however, might actually help in a small way to shape a more egalitarian and pluralistic climate of ethnic designation and, from that, of ethnic relations. For the same reason, the Reverend Jesse Jackson called for the abandonment of *black* in favor of *African American*. Names do matter in the social construction of reality, and these linguistic forms in some part can facilitate or impede social change.

Yet many people of various Latin-American backgrounds, including many middle class people with strong ethnic identities, now call themselves *Hispanics* with pride. Among Spanish-speaking Americans, *Hispanics* also signifies recognition of their common ethnic situation in this country, whatever their former diversity, and the bond of the language community.

A few other words have emerged in American English for the most oppressed and self-conscious segments of the largest national-origin groups among Hispanic Americans.

Chicano, and its feminine form *Chicana*, now have a firm niche in American English to denote Mexican Americans, especially those identified with ethnic nationalism and activism. The press and academic writers seem to be making a considerable effort to replace traditional terms, such as *Mexican American*, with *Chicano*, much as *black* replaced *Negro* in the late 1960s. *Chicano* is undoubtedly a good word for people both in and outside the group to denote those who identify with *Chicanismo* and *la raza*. No quarrel with that; *Chicano* is historically and ideologically fitting. But the effort to apply it as a collective term for all Americans of Mexican descent is questionable. The introduction of *Chicano* symbolizes the political and ideological polarization of the Mexican-American population and opens both terms to epithetical use.

For many years *Chicano* was a self descriptive used among the poor residents of the *barrios* in the American Southwest. While I have seen half a dozen fanciful folk etymologies, it is most likely that *Chicano* is simply a Mexican dialectal pronunciation of *Mexicano*, and this is probably correct. More precisely, it may be an Aztec or Nahuatl pronunciation. Most authorities, such as Edward R. Simmen (1969), agree. Lexicographers William and Mary Morris (1975) also believe this is the most probable origin, and quote Marcella Trujillo: "The word comes from the ending of the word 'Mexicano' as pronounced by the Aztecs and spelled by the Spaniards. The Aztecs pronounced the word 'Meschicano'. From the ending of the word came 'xicano' which was pronounced 'shicano' and which passed to 'chicano.' "

Chicano, as noted in Chapter 6, once had connotations of group self-disparagement in the *barrios*. It eventually became a term of class and status derogation that better-off, more assimilated Mexican Americans used against their poorer counterparts. By the familiar process of semantic inversion, *Chicano* in the late 1960s, like *black*, became a proud name preferred by younger, questioning, dissatisfied, politicized, vocal, and sometimes militant Mexican Americans. In the 1970s, *Chicanos* was widely adopted by the English-language press and by academics. (About the same time the Spanish *puertorriqueños, -as* came to be used in American English as a particularly sympathetic term for Puerto Ricans, the other large group of Hispanic Americans.)

With the appearance of *Chicano*, the traditional term *Mexican American* began to connote those older people who sought middle-class respectability and assimilation. From the Chicano viewpoint, the term *Mexican American* became a mild pejorative. The juxtaposition of *Chicano* to *Mexican American* has the same semantic relationship as *black* does to *Negro*, and those who preferred *Chicano* did not fail to see this parallel. Those blacks who were reluctant to let go of *Negro* in the late 1960s were labeled as *Uncle Toms* and, so, those who prefer traditional labels such as *Mexican American* are seen as *Tio Tacos* or, more to the point, as *Tio Tomases*. But *Chicano* has not spread as quickly among Mexican Americans as *black* did among African Americans.

More than a decade after the popular introduction of *Chicano*, it was still not the preferred label of most Mexican Americans. The Institute for Social Research at the University of Michigan in 1979 conducted a national survey of 976 Mexican Americans in which the respondents were asked to choose from among nine self-labels the one they preferred for their group. Myriam Torres (1983) informed me that only 10.1 percent chose the name *Chicano*. Almost eight of ten said they preferred either to be called *Mexicans* (56.7 percent), *Mexican Americans* (15.8 percent), or *Americans of Mexican descent* (6.7 percent)—all three being similar labels that stand in contrast to *Chicano*. More than twenty years ago, Edward R. Simmen (1969), who made a special study of the term, said that it was being accepted among educated *Mexican Americans* of responsible positions who had a special interest in improving the lot of the group. This is, I know, still true today. I read here and there that the term is gaining in popularity, but I suspect it is gaining more with trendy non-Mexicans in this country than it is with the referents themselves. This effort to make *Chicano* generic is in part responsible for opening the word to epithetical use.

Sociologist Philip E. Lampe in 1982 reported a scholarly study that examined the connotations of the terms *Chicano* and *Mexican American* in a sample of middle-class students attending private high schools in San Antonio. The sample was chosen to represent black, Mexican-American, and white non-Mexican students. Lampe reports that students of all ethnic backgrounds, and especially those of Mexican heritage, equated *Chicano* more often than *Mexican American* with negative traits. In effect, *Chicano* was used as an epithet. Private school students in San Antonio certainly are not representative of all Americans, yet I do hear the same pejorative or admiring uses, depending on who is saying the word. Lampe concludes that "contrary to what some may believe, the ethnic labels . . . *Chicano* and *Mexican American* are not merely alternative ways to name the same reality, but rather are indications of different realities." And finally he concludes: "Thus ethnic labels can be naming for some but can be name-calling for others."

By the mid-1970s many social scientists and journalists were using *Chicano* as a generic name for all Mexican Americans, regardless of their interest in ethnic politics. *Chicano* now appears in college textbooks on ethnic relations and social problems and is used synonymously and interchangeably with *Mexican American*, with *Chicano* increasingly getting the edge. Many ethnically conscious Mexicans and many academics and journalists of liberal disposition really want all people of Mexican heritage to be Chicanos so that the drama of the fight for ethnic equality, pluralism, and social justice can proceed without the complication of apathy in the ranks. The imposition of *Chicano* on all Mexican Americans is another case of well-intentioned people trying to create a more politically correct ethnic reality by renaming it.

The ethnic people of the Southern Appalachian region are now called *Appalachians* by many journalists and social scientists. Again, this is an adjective made into a new noun. An individual of this group, I suppose, would be called an *Appalachian*. The term obviously comes from the name of the Appalachian mountains, a range extending from Alabama to Quebec. The southern range of the mountains corresponds to the cultural region, which was settled in the late eighteenth and early nineteenth centuries by people of chiefly Scots-Irish, English, and Scots backgrounds.

The region, noted for its endemic rural poverty, became popularly known in the 1960s as "Appalachia." When the New Frontier of the Kennedy administration sent the Vista volunteers into the region, the long-standing fact of rural poverty was thrust into the popular mind. *Appalachia* came to symbolize indigenous poverty, and the poverty was and is real. Harry Caudill in his book *Night Comes to the Cumberlands* (1963), Robert Coles (1971), and others have documented the human toll of the region's poverty.

For a while in the early 1950s, social workers in the Ohio Valley and the Great Lakes urban regions called poor migrants from the southern hills *WASPS*, an acronym for (not what you think) *w*hite *A*ppalachian *S*outhern *P*rotestants. In Cincinnati the same people were called *SAMs*, *S*outhern *A*ppalachian *M*igrants. Imagine swarms of unemployed "WASPs" descending on the industrial cities of the Midwest; the name *SAMs* also has a derisive ring, for it is one of those common given names that so often become epithets for ethnic groups (see Chapter 3). Evidently, *Appalachians* is now the preferred term in the jargon of social science and social work.

The terms *Appalachia* and *Appalachians* do have certain historical precedents. Washington Irving once proposed *Appalachia* or *Alleghania* as a name for the nation. Horace Kephart, in his 1916 and now classic ethnographic study of the region, *Our Southern Highlanders*, used *Appalachia* as a name for the cultural area. John C. Campbell in his 1921 study of the region, *The Southern Highlander and His Home*, mused that if the region had become a "State of Appalachia" then the residents "would have been proud to call themselves 'Appalachians,' 'Southern Mountaineers,' or 'Southern Highlanders.' " But he did not otherwise use the name. As far as I know, the term *Appalachians* referring to the ethnic people of the region did not appear until the 1960s. *Appalachians*, in this new meaning of a people, does not appear in the 1961 third edition of the Merriam-Webster unabridged dictionary. Bowing to trendy academic usage, in 1980 the *Harvard Encyclopedia of American Ethnic Groups* adopted *Appalachians* for its entry on upland Southerners.

Appalachians, as everyone knows, refers mainly to the working- and lower-class hill folk, and for that reason it is another euphemism tilting toward a codeword. The contrived term *Appalachians* stigmatizes the rural poor of the region with the idea of poverty popularly associated with "Appalachia." Most of the people in the region in fact are not poor, and it is clear that the term does not apply to them. These so-called Appalachians are of course one and the same as "hillbillies," a slur for the group dating from about 1900. In the 1950s, *hillbillies* was inverted to positive, jocular use within the group. And I will not be the first to point out that the rural poor of the region do not often live *on* the hills but usually *in* the hollows *between* the hills.

Appalachians, because of its identity with rural poverty and its largely uncomplimentary denotation of the quasi-ethnic group of the region, holds the potential of both an ethnic and a class slur. Better, more traditional terms are available. Horace Kephart, and, a little later, John C. Campbell used the graceful term *Southern Highlanders* for the ethnic people of the Southern Appalachians. That term is elegant, descriptive, and accurate with no sly pejoration. Yet the ethnic culture of the Southern uplands is but a variant of Southern culture, so the term *Appalachian Southerners* could and sometimes has served equally well.

TERMS THAT BEGAN AS CODEWORDS

Another, related class of names for ethnic groups is those that hatch as mature codewords. These terms are not high-minded euphemisms but are more like slang and common slurs. The harsher ethnic slurs are now seldom heard in polite company. The common slurs that survive in the language are heard mostly in rough street vernacular, vicious teenage talk, and animal-house college slang—and from naughty children and unrepentant, shameless adult bigots. But a few sly slurs fall halfway between the euphemisms and mild codewords already discussed in this chapter and rough common slurs. I am pleased to report that most are antiques.

Paradoxically, most codewords for ethnic groups are transparent, and that fact too has its uses. Most non-Jewish Americans are aware of the historical concentration of Jews in the City of New York and its suburbs, including suburban New Jersey. Other groups have since become as numerous, but the near equation of living in the City and being Jewish is still strong in the popular mind. The terms *New Yorker* and *city type*, at least a few years ago, were codewords for Jews. *City boy* is another codeword for a Jew, and it slyly suggests *Jew boy*, an overt slur. The punning word play of *Jew Nork* and even a suburban *Jew Nersey* leave little doubt.

Hyphenated American, a term originating in the late nineteenth century, is a mild epithet for an ethnic person, especially from the first generation or two of immigrants, who maintains two identities—that of a national ethnic person and that of an American national. The word *hyphenated* refers to the hyphen in the terms, such as *Italian-American*, *Jewish-American*, *Polish-American*, *Mexican-American*, *Chinese-American*, *German-American* (I don't often hear *British-American*; they seem to become Americans at once—or stay British forever!). *Hyphenated-American* clearly was used as a codeword for a "foreigner," "immigrant," or such. Subsequent slang forms testify to the pejoration.

Maurice Weseen, who compiled a widely cited dictionary of slang in the 1930s, reported that a *hyphenate* (*hyphen*, for short) was a person of "divided allegiance," especially in wartime. (I presume he was alluding to the ambivalence of some German-Americans before the First World War.) *Hyphenism*, reports Weseen, is such "a division of allegiance between two countries, especially in wartime."

Hyphenate and *hyphenism* apparently later lost their connotations of disloyalty. These slangy terms eventually made their way into academic writing. For example, they appeared in 1964—and completely without pejoration—in the title and text of a scholarly book, *The Hyphenate in Recent American Politics and Diplomacy*, by Louis L. Gerson, a political scientist, and they have been elsewhere and more recently used.

Recently, I have seen a few inverted or positive uses of *hyphenated American* to refer collectively to persons of relatively recent immigrant groups who still maintain two identities, that of an ethnic person and that of an American citizen—with no disloyalty implied. Being a so-called hyphenated American became a respectable identity during the white ethnic revival of the early 1970s. This is another instance of a word, which began as an offensive epithet, coming full circle in meaning.

At least one other old sly slur bears mention. Families who immigrated from Eastern and Southern Europe and from Spanish-speaking countries often have surnames that end in vowels—*a, e, i, o, u* and sometimes *y*. People used to speak disparagingly of a person from one of these groups as *one of those names that end in a vowel*.

A FEW FOR THE MAJORITIES

The popular resurgence of minority ethnicity and the penitent atmosphere in majority groups since the 1960s made it more acceptable for minority-group members to slur majorities. Majority-group targets, especially if they are feeling guilty, are often willing to take their lumps, for it all seems socially just, considering the lamentable history of their relations with minority groups.

WASPs, the well-known acronym for *w*hite Anglo-Saxon Protestants, when used in some contexts, is clearly a codeword for "Protestant." *WASP* is used mostly in the Northeast and Middle West with respect to the relations between white Protestant majorities and Jewish and Catholic minorities. The verbal antagonism of some intellectuals of minority background toward the Protestant Establishment has to do, among other things, with old religious resentments. The acronym *WASPs* avoids the overt use of the word *Protestants* in antagonistic contexts, which might invite the words *Catholics* and *Jews* in response and draw into relief the troublesome element of religious differences—a near taboo in polite ethnic conflict. *WASP* in other ways is one of the most ingenious of codewords, with several layers of covert meaning. I devote the entirety of chapter 10 to the sting of *WASP*.

In the Southwest the tension is between Mexican Americans and other, non-Mexican Americans. *Anglo* is an item of Mexican American slang dating from the 1940s that refers to non-Mexican-Americans, especially those of "Anglo-Saxon" background. The name *Anglo* is from the combining form *Anglo-*, which means of or pertaining to things English. *Anglo* also suitably suggests *Anglophone*, a term that is coming to be used for one who speaks English in a non-English-speaking community. But *Anglo* is just a nickname for almost all non-Mexicans, one of those "them" versus "us" words. Expectably, *Anglo* is also now used for white non-Cubans in Miami. Stuart Berg Flexner, in his book *I Hear America Talking* (1976), suggests that *Anglo* was originally offensive. Yet the term has been taken up by English-speaking Americans as a self descriptive. *Anglo* is now appearing in sociology textbooks and other academic writing, which has proved so receptive to other codewords and euphemisms.

CHAPTER 9

ACRIMONIOUS ACRONYMS

MANY DEROGATORY NICKNAMES for ethnic groups, both minority and majority, are various kinds of word play, such as puns, Pig Latin, blends, alterations, clippings, reduplications, and other devices. The acronym (for example *SAM*, for *S*outhern *A*ppalachian *M*igrant in the industrial cities of Ohio) and its cousin, the initialism (as in *P. R.*, for *P*uerto *R*ican), are among the newest devices for forming nicknames for ethnic groups in the slang of North American English. I have found a score of these terms for American ethnic groups. Almost all now appear in the *Acronyms, Initialisms, and Abbreviations Dictionary*, the major listing of these terms in American usage.

H. L. Mencken once noted the American inclination for "reducing complex concepts to starkest abbreviations." The word *acronym* first appeared in dictionaries in the 1940s and derives from the transliterated Greek *akros* for tip and *onyma* for name. Thus, acronyms are formed from the "tips" or initial letters of a name.

Acronyms, while an old device, became famous as names of the "alphabet soup" agencies of the New Deal and from military use in the Second World War. Organizations, industrial processes, and many other things are now named so

that the acronym spells something pronounceable , prefera-
bly with one syllable. At their most inventive, acronyms spell
a word that alludes to an attribute of the named thing, such
as *WASP* (*W*omen's *A*irforce *S*ervice *P*ilots, Second World
War, for all wasps fly). Long, cumbersome proper names are
sometimes given just so the acronym will spell something
catchy and mnemonic, such as *MOUSE* (*M*inimal *O*rbital
*U*nmanned *S*atellite of *E*arth). Many acronyms have entered
the language as words and their acronymic origins are half
forgotten, such as *SNAFU* (Second World War slang for *S*it-
uation *N*ormal—*A*ll *F*ucked *U*p and at least a dozen variants).

Acronyms are especially amenable to use as slang and slurs.
An acronym can denote its referent, and, in addition, it can
be devised to characterize it by the connotation of the word
spelled. Some acronyms for ethnic groups also have the pejorative sound connotations that mark derogating words in
English.

The early acronyms for ethnic groups probably were coined
by social workers and social scientists to refer to their "clients"
and "subjects" in a way that seemed scientific. *SAM* (*S*outhern *A*ppalachian *M*igrant), *WASP* (*W*hite *A*ppalachian
*S*outhern *M*igrant, and then later and independently, *w*hite
*A*nglo-*S*axon *P*rotestant), the initialisms *P. R.* (*P*uerto *R*ican)
and *ABC* (*A*merican-*b*orn *C*hinese), and others probably
originated in this way. This professional jargon quickly passed
into the locutions of pop sociology, where it took on epithetical overtones and became slang.

The earliest acronym for an ethnic group I have found
originated in social studies. *WIN* was coined in 1926 by Arthur H. Estabrook and I. E. McDougle for their racist book
Mongrel Virginians: The Win Tribe. *WIN* apparently stands
for *w*hite, *I*ndian, *N*egro, although the authors nowhere ad-
mit this trite invention. This pronounceable acronymic shell
was a pseudonym for a rural community of racially mixed
persons whom social scientists now call "tri-racial isolates."

WIN is the only permutation of the three initial letters that spells anything.

HATCHLINGS OF *WASP*

It was not until the 1960s and the spate of ethnic consciousness that acronymic nicknames for ethnic groups became popular. *WASP* (*w*hite Anglo-Saxon Protestant) was the first and most influential. It deserves a close look because its success as slang made it the model for others. More important, the history of the WASP acronym is a remarkably vivid example of how and why ethnic epithets enter the language. I have devoted the entirety of the next, final chapter of this one word, which is still enjoying the bloom of youth and respectability.

WASP, one of the best buzzwords of the 1960s and 1970s, became the model for imitators. *WASC* (*w*hite Anglo-Saxon Catholic) has been used for English Catholic communities in Kentucky and Maryland. Joan Cooper (1978), a social worker, coined *WECC* (*w*hite English Celtic Catholic) to call attention to another Catholic minority from the British Isles. In Canada, *QWASP* (Quebec *w*hite Anglo-Saxon Protestant) has hatched from the conflict between the Anglo-Canadians and the Quebeckers. *TOM*, according to John Robert Colombo (1979), is an acronym for a Canadian national elite, predominately Anglophones, who seem to concentrate in Toronto, Ottawa, and Montreal. *TOM* also suggests *tom* and *tommy*, which are old nicknames for the British.

There are yet other spinoffs of *WASP*. In the 1960s, a few blacks scolded other, assimilating blacks as *NASPs* (Negro "Anglo-Saxon" Protestants), which is roughly equivalent to *uncle tom*, *afro-saxon*, or *oreo*. The scolding of Jewish assimilators, it has been attested to me, resulted in *WASH* (White Anglo-Saxon Hebrews). Florence King (1977) used *HASP* (Hebrew Anglo-Saxon Protestant) in the same sense in her satirical book on "WASPs." *BOWP* (*b*lack *o*rdinary *w*orking *p*eople) is listed in Crowley (1982), but she says in a private correspondence that it may be a nonce word.

Slang from the world of the physically disabled gives us *WASPA* (*w*hite Anglo-*S*axon *P*rotestant *a*mbulatory) as a bitter comment upon what is required to get a job. Ethel Strainchamps (1971, 244), a lexicographer, editor, and feminist, by way of fixing blame for epithets for women, coined *WASMs* (*w*hite Anglo-*S*axon *m*ales). And, according to writer Paul Dickson (1982), the Protestants get it again with *WUMP* (*W*hite *U*rban *M*iddle-class *P*rotestants). The last word is yet another *WASP*, reportedly an ephemeral item of Israeli slang in the early 1970s, for *w*hite *A*shkenazic *S*abra with *p*ull.

Yet the most bizarre acronym prompted by *WASP* is *PIGS* (*P*oles, *I*talians, *G*reeks, and *S*lavs), which was presented, if not coined, by Michael Novak (1971) in his book *The Rise of the Unmeltable Ethnics.* Some in the white ethnic movement apparently felt a need for an acronymic protagonist against the *WASPs*. If the *WASPs* were the "un-ethnics," then who were the real "ethnics," acronymically speaking? Mostly, he says, they are *P*oles, *I*talians, *G*reeks, and *S*lavs. (The more assimilated Irish were kept out of this acronymic *PIG*-sty, perhaps also because they would ruin the spelling.) The ordering of the group names is not by alphabet, group size, or any other ranking; it merely spells something useful in political rhetoric. Abrahams and Kalčik (1978) write that the term *PIGS* "is an insulting self-polluting label, and [is] the claim to belong to the margins of society rather than to be part of the center or establishment [and] also reverses the assimilation process and brings down on the ethnics' heads the charge of being different, non-Anglo." *PIGS* never caught on and apparently died a quiet death, perhaps never leaving the pages of Novak's book.

An ingroup joke, the famous notion of the Jewish Princess, in the 1970s was acronymized on the campuses as *JAP* for *J*ewish-*A*merican *P*rincess. The hyphenated -*American* was added, I presume, to give a vowel and make it spell something. The kids sometimes plugged in *Prince* to make the acronym do double duty. *JAP* is now in general, national slang and the stereotype of the Jewish Princess is so popular that two self-satirizing books about *JAPS*—spoiled, grasping, Daddy's girls—were published in 1982.

INITIALISMS

I have found several initialisms that refer to ethnic persons. While an acronym is usually pronounced as a word, an initialism is pronounced letter by letter. Mencken reported the earliest initialism that I have found. *F. M. C.*, *free man of color*, was used by and, later, for freed blacks. A. R. Dunlap and C. A. Weslager (1947), writing in *American Speech*, relate that the *G*-and-*B* Indians, a settlement of "tri-racial isolates," got their name from living near the *G*rafton and *B*elington Railroad. *P. R.* for *Puerto Rican* appeared in the 1950s or 1960s, at a time when migrants to the mainland were settling heavily in the cities and were a concern to social workers, who perhaps originated the initialism. The old epithet *house nigger* for a black sycophant in the late 1960s was euphemized and coded to *h. n.* Working in the other direction, *jaybee*, a derogatory nickname for a black person, is a phonetic spelling, ironically modeled on *Jaycee*, of the initialism *j. b.* for *jet black*.

BLEND WORDS

Blend words, which make a new word from syllables of usually two words, are related in form and spirit to acronyms and initialisms. When the proper names of ethnic groups are re-formed in this way, the new words often seem to diminish the referents, just as acronyms do. Yet blends for ethnic groups appear now and then, usually coined by social scientists and other well-meaning sorts. An early blend was *Aframerican* (*Afr*ican and *American*) and during the Second World War *Filamerican* (*Fil*ipino and *American*) was proposed.

Most recent blends have to do with seeking a new name for Native Americans, who understandably sometimes object to the names *Indians* and *American Indians*, pointing out they are not "Indians" (a name resulting from white people's ignorance) but are the original, native Americans. These indigenous peoples by the 1970s were at least 173 different ethnic groups, each having a proper name. When they are referred to collectively, many prefer to be called *Native Americans*. The *N* in *Native Americans* is usually capitalized to set the referents apart from *n*ative Americans, or anyone native-born in the United States. *Natives* with a capital initial is sometimes used as a short form. *Natam* from *Nat*ive *Am*erican appeared in the 1970s. According to H. L. Mencken, *Amerindian* was proposed in 1899 and was soon shortened to *Amerind*; the latter was revived in the 1970s and found favor with some social scientists.

FOLK ETYMOLOGIES

The general awareness of acronyms has spawned a new line of free association in spurious or folk etymologies. As linguist Sterling Eisiminger (1978) points out, nowadays when people do not know the origin of a word, they sometimes imagine that it must be an acronym. At least three well-known slurs for ethnic groups are widely but mistakenly believed to derive from acronyms. A popular story has it that *wop* for an Italian is an acronym for *W*ith-*o*ut *P*apers (or sometimes *P*assport) and was applied to illegal immigrants who were deported in the 1920s. Another story has *wop* as an acronym for the phrase *W*ork(s) *o*n *P*avement, which is probably suggested by the occupational stereotype of Italians as concentrated in masonry and road-building. But etymologists seem in wide agreement that *wop* is a clipped and phonetically spelled version of Neapolitan and Sicilian *guappo*, a daring, handsome man—a dude.

A similar belief is that *wog* comes from an acronym for Wonderful (sometimes Wily) Oriental Gentleman. No one really knows the origin of *wog*, but Merriam III says it may be a variant of *golliwog*, the name of a grotesque black doll in a children's story. *Pome* and its diminutive form *pommy* are apparently nicknames for Anglo-Australians, as well as the more familiar Australian name for an Englishman or the English in general. Crowley relates one possibility that *pome* is an acronym for Prisoner Of Mother England, supposedly a nickname for a convict in a nineteenth-century penal colony in Australia. She also relates a second hypothesis that *pome* is short for *pomegranate*, a red fruit, and alludes to the sunburn that fair-skinned Englishmen often acquired on arrival in Australia. The prisoner story is highly unlikely, though the pomegranate story has some possibility and is similar to one of several possibilities of the origin on *pommy* given by Eric Partridge.

The urge to explain mysterious etymologies of popular words of slang as acronyms seems near universal. In the Soviet Union a caste of tramps wander over Siberia and are known as *bichi*. Serge Schmemann (1981) writing in *The New York Times* says, "The name derives from 'beachcomber,' but the popular explanation is that it comes from the Russian initials for 'former intelligent person.' "

TWO CURIOSITIES

Paki, the slur-name for Pakistani immigrants in Britain, Canada, and the United States, is clipped from *Pakistani*. *Paki* is an instance of an ethnic epithet, which was coined only as a derisive short form, but unbeknown to its users it is in fact originally an acronym. William and Mary Morris (1977) note the curiosity that *Pakistan* is an acronym created in 1933 and adopted as the official name of the state after the Second World War. It is "made up of the first or last letters of a group of other words. Thus *Pakistan* contains these elements: *P* for Punjab; *A* for the Afghan border states; *K* for Kashmir; *S* for Sind; and *tan* for Baluchistan. By what is certainly more than just a happy coincidence, *Pakistan* is also composed of the Persian root *pak*, meaning 'pure, unadulterated or holy,' and *stan*, a common Urdu suffix meaning 'land or place.' "

In conclusion, I will relate another curiosity whereby an initialism, in a roundabout way, may have given birth to the nickname *charlie* for the Vietnamese in the Vietnam War. Stuart Berg Flexner in *I Hear America Talking* (1976) reports that *charlie* is derived from the initialism *V. C.* for *Viet Cong*, the short form of the Vietnamese phrase meaning "Vietnamese Communists." They were simply called *the Cong*. *Viet Cong* was also abbreviated to *V. C.* The military communication code word for *V* is *Victor* and for *C* is *Charlie*. So the Viet Cong or the V. C. were called *Victor Charlie* or simply *charlie*, corresponding to the short form *Cong*. I will add that this usage may have been reinforced by the coincidence that *charlie* is also an old slur for several Asian groups, including the Vietnamese.

Nicknames for ethnic groups formed on acronyms and initialisms are just the newest wrinkle in the old game of intergroup name-calling. Certainly, others are around in the streets—and in the groves of Academe.

CHAPTER 10

DING, DONG, THE WICKED WASP IS DEAD

IN THE EARLY 1970s when the white ethnic revival got under way, the ethnic intellectuals and others who bandy pop sociology in the mass media of the land declared the rise of the unmeltable "ethnics" and the decline of the so-called *WASPs*—the acronym for *w*hite *A*nglo-*S*axon *P*rotestants. Those were heady times, frothy enough to inspire critic Alfred Kazin in 1972 to tell a group of New York college students that "if any group is to be pitied, it is perhaps the 'Wasps,' who find their books reviewed on the back pages of *The New York Times Book Review*" (quoted by Johnson, 1972).

As some of the intellectuals see it, the "WASPs" are like, as Nancy Mitford (1955) said of an aristocracy in a republic, "a chicken whose head has been cut off: it may run about in a lively way, but in fact it is dead." In this final chapter, the natural history of the epithet *WASP* tells a story of ethnic relations played out in the print media.

WASP is one of those pronounceable and irresistible acronyms that has found a firm niche in the American language since it appeared in the mid-1950s. As a new word of slang, probably originating in social science, *WASP* was embraced at once by journalists, literary intellectuals, and social critics. *WASP* is a model of a life history of an ethnic slur. It is today enjoying its latest wave of popularity and a certain respectability in print and speech, as *kike, wop, darky,* and other slurs did ninety years ago. John Higham (1975), the eminent historian of Protestant America, noted that by the 1960s *WASP* was the only ethnic slur that could be safely used in polite company, for the name was considered part of a socially just assault on certain bastions of ethnic exclusiveness.

The success of *WASP* in American slang is a joy to behold. It is a naughty and funny word that almost everyone, including me, finds an occasion to use. *WASP* is slang in that prime sense of denoting a referent and also characterizing it in aggressive, reproving, metaphorical, and manifold ways. And the WASPs themselves have taken up the term, often becoming the best satirists of their own customs and folkways. It is always funnier when the butts play themselves.

The first major dictionary to list *WASP* was the *Random House Dictionary* in 1966, and it labeled the term "often derogatory." (The second edition of 1987 under the editorship of Stuart Berg Flexner changed the label to "sometimes disparaging and offensive.") The next to list it was the 1970 *American Heritage Dictionary*, which gave it a literary gloss with a quotation from Norman Mailer: "The Wasps have taken power." Later dictionaries and supplements also list the term but most do not label it "derogatory" or "slang." Nonetheless, Stuart Berg Flexner lists *WASP* in the 1975 Second Supplemented Edition of the *Dictionary of American Slang* and notes its often derogatory use. Flexner, elsewhere in the Supplement, defines *Barbie Doll* as a "typical all-American conformist, esp. a 'WASP'; a dehumanized person." *WASP*, in its connotations, has all the earmarks of an ethnic epithet—it disparages, it ridicules, and it stereotypes.

WASP is a buzzword for a generation of social critics. As a term of pop sociology, *WASP* is the spiritual heir of the epithets *bourgeois* in the 1930s and 1940s and *suburban* in the 1950s and 1960s. It connotes the coincidence of class privilege, suburban conformity, and the smugness of majority ethnicity—all rolled into one word. Many literary critics and newspaper and magazine columnists use it straight and unapologetically. Curiously, its use in media seems confined to print intended for "segmented" audiences; I have only rarely heard it used in scripted TV shows, perhaps because it is well understood as a slur and may offend some in a general audience. In the 1983 cult movie *Liquid Sky*, the heroine was called "a WASP cunt from Connecticut." In earlier, negative reactions to ethnic diversity in America, other ethnic slurs were similarly accepted as good, straight reporting.

THE BIRTH OF *WASP*

WASP, like most slang, is a child of its time. *WASP* was first heard in the mid-1950s, coincident with a surge of popular questioning of inequality in American society. The first known printed use of *WASP* was in 1957 by Andrew Hacker in the *American Political Science Review* (pp. 1009–26). He was clearly referring to those of the wealthy establishment, especially in the East (Shapiro 1989). The term became widely known in social science after the publication in 1964 of E. Digby Baltzell's *The Protestant Establishment*.[1] The historian John Higham points out what is perhaps the earliest literary use. Saul Bellow in *Herzog*, published in 1964, has Moses Herzog ruminating on his defiance of "the Wasps, who. . . stopped boiling their own soap circa 1880, took European tours, and began to complain of the Micks and the Spicks and the Sheenies" (p. 377).

A curious little mystery surrounds the ultimate origin of the term. Originally, there were two *WASPs*. By the mid-1950s, *WASP* was Chicago slang and Ohio Valley social workers' jargon for *w*hite *A*ppalachian *S*outhern *P*rotestant.

These *WASPs* were the poor whites who migrated to and settled in enclaves in the industrial cities of northern Ohio and the Great Lakes region after the Second World War. I also heard the acronym with this referent in the 1950s among social workers in the Southern Appalachians who used it as a form-filling shorthand. By 1960, the other, more familiar *WASP* (for *w*hite *A*nglo-*S*axon *P*rotestant) emerged and the hillbilly *WASP* buzzed off. The middle-class suburban *WASP* has swept the field, and few know that the same acronym first referred to the poor country cousins of the Establishment *WASPs*. While I suspect the two *WASPs* are cases of independent evolution, it is conceivable that, like a hermit crab, the latter inhabited the shell of the former.

WASP had a lazy, remote existence during the first decade of its life. *WASP* began to emerge as a slur in the late 1960s. During the Civil Rights Movement the term was used by white liberals to denote the Protestant Establishment in this country, and I suspect that *WASP* began to take on its present range of connotations about that time. But it was not until the early 1970s that *WASP* emerged as a studied epithet, and I believe this was associated with the nostalgic wave of white ethnic identity—"the rise of the unmeltable ethnics."

New words appear in a language, and in this case also take on new meanings, when they usefully denote a "new" category of social reality that was previously of less or of no use to define. Peter Schrag's 1971 *The Decline of the WASP* and Michael Novak's 1972 *The Rise of the Unmeltable Ethnics* made rhetoric of the new ethnic ideology, and the idea of the WASP was the pivot. Most social movements, and ethnic identity movements are no exception, develop an ideology to explain what the movement is seeking or is rejecting, to explain the social injustices of the past and present, to identify devils and scapegoats, and to generate solidarity in the movement of defining a hostile, monolithic outgroup. For some of the ideological spokesmen for the white "ethnics," the outgroup is the WASPs. The WASPs became, for the "ethnics," what sociologists call a "negative reference group" or a standard from which the "ethnics" sought to disaffiliate.

WHO ARE THE WASPs?

WASP originally referred to the historical white Protestant elites or Establishment in this country and to their ideology. To that extent the term denoted however inexactly a highly pertinent idea. E. Digby Baltzell, in *The Protestant Establishment* (1964), used the acronym to describe the elite segment or caste of white Protestants who dominated American power and culture well into the twentieth century. Baltzell seems to use the term mainly as an adjective. Sociologists originally used the term not so much to refer to a certain stock of Americans but to the historically dominant culture, language, and customs in this country, especially perhaps that brand that emanated from New England. *WASP* denoted historically and culturally dominant elements in American society, namely, whiteness, a doctrine or an assumption of the superiority of Anglo-Saxon culture and traditions, and Protestantism. *WASP*, then, denoted an important residual category of multi-ethnic reality in American life having a common denominator of Protestant inclinations, however diverse. The appearance of some such term was probably inevitable.

But popular usage, and also that of journalists, intellectuals, and social scientists, fell into one of the most common traps in thinking about society. *WASP* originally indicated a useful abstraction. The abstract noun soon emerged in usage as a concrete one. That is, users fell into the error of reification and came to use the term to denote a material category of persons and to suggest that such persons constitute

an ethnic monolith with certain stereotypical social and behavioral traits.

At face value, *WASP* denotes white Protestants of Anglo-
Saxon or more generally of British Isles background, especially descendents of early immigrants. The term was quickly
extended to Protestants of North European descent—Germans, Dutch, Scandinavians. And *WASP* can wing further.
Diane Johnson, reviewing Saul Bellow's *The Dean's December* in *The New York Review* (1982), wrote: "It's hard to re-
member that Corde himself is a WASP, a Huguenot from a
distinguished old family. He and his family seem like nice
Jewish characters, as usual." *WASP* is a catch-all for a variegated, originally polyglot, regionally diverse category of white
Americans who have some kind of connection, often nomi-
nal, with scores of Protestant denominations and sects. A
WASP, then, is almost any English-speaking American who
is not Catholic, Orthodox, or Jewish, or of African or Asian
descent.

Insofar as *WASP* refers to all white Protestants, and this
is clearly one of its uses, it designates little or no social reality. The ideological urge is to identify white Protestants as
a kind of unethnic ethnic group, a relative monolith of reli-
gion, ideology, custom, behavior, association, and common
interest, so they can be identified in the field, labeled, and
generalized about. An ethnic epithet is a stereotype of an
outgroup, and *WASP* is an exceedingly crude stereotype. The
epithet takes no account of the variety of national and linguistic white Protestant origins or of distinctive, home-grown
regional cultures that have developed over many genera-
tions. The stereotype lumps New England "Yankees," Appalachian Southerners, Scots Presbyterians, Mormons,
Swedish Lutherans, the Amish, Tennessee Scotch-Irish,
Missouri Synod Lutherans, the Pennsylvania Dutch, white
Southern Baptists, Huguenots, and a variety of other groups
under the single rubric *WASP*.

Much of the ethnic variety among white Protestants is

among the rural and lower-income segments, but not all of it. This relative invisibility of the poor white Protestants may account for some of the tendency of ethnically self-conscious intellectuals to see the middle-class white Protestants in the cities and suburbs of the Northeast and Midwest as a relative ethnic monolith. These social critics also tend to view the scores of Protestant denominations and sects in this country as a kind of un-Catholic church. Sociologist William B. Helmreich in his 1982 book *The Things They Say Behind Your Back* struggled to define the reality of the WASPs that is characterized by the stereotypes of white Protestants in our national and ethnic folklore. Admitting to their great diversity of national origin, regional culture, class, and ideology, Helmreich nonetheless asserted that they are "a distinct entity" because they share "a common Protestant faith." What common Protestant faith?

Since *WASP* refers to any and all white Protestants in this country, why are they not just called "white Protestants," which is precisely denotative? Very simple, I think. The users want to avoid saying the word *Protestant*. *WASP* serves a certain euphemistic purpose as well as being an epithet. The term *WASP* avoids the appearance of religious or sectarian confrontation, which may invite the words *Jew* and *Catholic* in response, and then we would be back at that old business. *WASP* is a way to avoid saying "middle-class Protestants" just as *ethnics* is a way to avoid saying "working-class Catholics." The principals in the discussion of white ethnic revival, who first popularized the term *WASP*, are intellectuals of various minority backgrounds who have made it. The discussion is really about recalling the injuries of class and cultural resentment. Perhaps *WASP* helps to focus the discussion on those issues while avoiding the appearance of sectarian name-calling, which it also is. But more often *WASPs* is a mealy-mouthed word for "Protestants," usually middle-class ones.

THE ANATOMY OF *WASP*

Did the coinage of *WASP* have anything to do with a delightfully and identically spelled wasp—the irascible insect? Certainly. But allowing the possibility of coincidence, it was a happy and useful one. *Wasp* has long been a metaphor for an irritable, disagreeable person and *waspish* is the adjective that describes such traits. Part of the stereotype of the WASP is that of having a dour, humorless, driven, emotionless disposition. Oh, what a happy convergence of three images!— the spelling, the reputation of the insect, and the stereotype. Entirely expectedly, the adjectives *waspish* and *waspy* appeared immediately to characterize *WASP*-like persons and things, and the *American Heritage Dictionary* and others quickly lent authority to these new words. Then came the nouns *waspishness, waspism, waspdom, waspland,* and the *Time*-spun (17 January 1969, 25) *waspirant* (for a social-climbing "ethnic"). And I have seen the verb *wasped* (to make WASP-like) and the adverb *waspily*. William Safire (1989) in his syndicated column "On Language" recently gave us *Waspism,* meaning a locution peculiar to the ethnic vernacular of WASPs.

The people who use *WASP* in all seriousness seem to be comfortable, even satisfied, with the redundancy of white and Anglo-Saxon. It would seem bizarre to refer to "white Irish Catholics," for example. Actually, it would make more sense for "Anglo-Saxon" to modify "white" (*ASWP*) than vice versa, but that would not spell anything.[2] Back when *WASP* was first chic, member wags logically suggested that the tautological *WASP* ought to be simply *ASP*, which is equally pronounceable and connotes a creature of equally bad reputation. But they missed the point that the redundancy is the key to the pejorative connotation and the rhetorical force of *WASP*. *ASP* just doesn't have the same sting. Nonetheless, *ASP* had a brief life in the late 1960s and was recorded by Barnhart's 1973 dictionary of new English. *WASP* soon got an initialism, *NN*, tacked on as a kind of tail stinger. Perry Weed (1973) wrote: "The largest minority is the so-called 'WASP-NN,' that is, White Anglo-Saxon Protestant Native born of Native parents." But that was stretching a point, and it was never heard from again.

The redundancy of white and Anglo-Saxon has just the connotation intended. The reiteration recalls and is intended to remind of the present and historical whiteness of a "group" that has long dominated power and culture in American society. And the reiteration of whiteness in combination with Anglo-Saxonism also associates this "group," quite accurately, with slavery, racism, anti-Catholicism, Nativism, theories of Anglo-Saxon superiority, and attempts to foist Anglo-Saxon culture and values onto more recent immigrant groups.

John Ciardi, in *A Second Browser's Dictionary* (1983), repeats a suggestion that *WERSP* (White Erse Protestant) would be historically a sounder term. *Erse*, from the Scottish, means "Gaelic," especially Scottish Gaelic. Ciardi is right insofar as descendants of Celtic groups in colonial America, chiefly the Scotch-Irish and fewer Scots, became in the nineteenth century some of the most fierce Nativists. Perhaps *WERSP* is most fitting for Southern "WASPs" who are probably more Scots-Irish than Anglo-Saxon, while white Protestants in New England are more likely to be Anglo-Saxon or English in ancestry.

I discussed at the end of Chapter 7 how in the 1970s the usage of *WASP*, like certain other ethnic epithets, had at times slid by stages into lower case, from *WASP*, to *Wasp*, and occasionally down to *wasp*, a literatum "decline of the WASP." A true acronym, as its users insist it is and nothing more, would have to remain in all upper case. Lately journalistic usage seems to be standardizing on an all upper case form and fewer *Wasps* and *wasps* have been seen.

Journalists now and then pump up the acronym and re-

view the current status of the WASPs and usually find it
deflated. In a 1983 feature story, Sid Moody of the Associated Press asked: "WASP: Are you losing thy sting?" He
quotes the society historian Cleveland Amory: "I don't think
the *P* is too important nowadays, anyway. But without the
P we're just *WAS*, and that's not very comforting." The "decline of the *WASP*" is now a cultural cliché in the wide audience who enjoy ritual enactments. The successful comedy
playwright A. R. Gurney, Jr., himself a WASP, has come to
preside over theatrical treatments about pratfalls of the
WASPs (Witchel 1989). Gurney's perceptive "pointing up"
of WASP character and manners delights theater audiences,
not unlike the broad ethnic stereotypes of vaudeville routines did at the turn of the century. The ethnic humor is
especially gratifying to ethnic others and even seems au-
thenticated when it comes from an ethnic insider.

But the journalistic establishment is not oblivious to the
fact that *WASP* is an old-fashioned ethnic slur and carries a
crude stereotype. *The New York Times* recently allowed the
essayist and novelist Edward Hoagland to air this curmud-
geonly view in an "Op-Ed" piece; "WASP Stings. It Isn't
Amusing," and he made the point unflinchingly. A few weeks
later *The New York Times* printed the predictable letter of
response: The white Anglo-Saxon Protestants have been
beating up on minorities for a long time, so it is understand-
able and forgiveable that such a slur would emerge. Indeed,
and why not?

FUN WITH *WASP*

The success of *WASP* as a derogatory name for the white
Protestant Establishment lies in its capacity for playful du-
plicity. Denotatively, it is just a "sociological" descriptive
for the racial, national-origin, and religious traits of the historically and culturally dominant ethnic groups in North

America. Connotatively, it conjures up a whole laundry list of things many intellectuals hate.

Back in the early 1970s, journalists and critics in the Eastern press had a heyday with the *WASP* handle. WASPs were declared fair game and WASP-baiting became a sport. WASP jokes began to appear, tit for tat, to match the Italian and Polish jokes, which seem unsinkable. The chickens had come home to roost and the WASPs were getting their epithetical comeuppance. A 1971 article by Mel Watkins in *The New York Times Book Review* is an example of systematic WASP-baiting. Mr. Watkins had a bit of satirical fun imagining what book titles might appear to accompany a fantastic WASP ethnic identity movement. The whole stereotype was there, including three or four allusions to WASP racism and bigotry, and among the punning book titles—*Wasp Nests: Enclaves in the Urban Ghetto*.

A few years later, as the ethnic revival discussion perked along, *New York* magazine (1974) had a cover illustrated with a picture of a Wall Street type replete with wasp wings and a tail stinger. Owen Edwards, author of the cover story, "The New York Wasp Is Not an Endangered Species," plays and puns on the acronym. The wave of anti-WASP chic in the magazines moved Robert Claiborne in a 1974 *Newsweek* essay to deny the stereotype and defend "Wasp values." By 1978, Russell Baker was poking fun at the stereotype, protesting that he was a *GASP* (Grey Anglo-Saxon Protestant).

Florence King, a white Southerner and a WASP insider, gave us the best satire on the WASPs in her 1977 book, *WASP, Where Is Thy Sting?* She insists that "stereotyping, better known as 'perceptive pointing up,' is an ancient and honorable ingredient of the humorous literary genre." King, outrageous as usual, works over the idiosyncratic folkways of mostly middle-class white Protestants, with a bias toward the Southern wing. She does this, unlike the media intellectuals, without ever getting serious. The ethnic ideologues, on the other hand, are earnest about this stuff. Throughout the 1970s and into the 1980s the stereotype became simpler and more pointed.

PERSONALITY OF *WASP*

WASP, in the hands of the intellectuals and academics, quickly came to stand, as John Higham noted, for a "desiccated, life-denying culture." Wilfred Sheed in 1972 reviewed Peter Schrag's *The Decline of the WASP* and Novak's *The Rise of the Unmeltable Ethnics* and commented that both authors "suggest that white Protestants are so stiff with inner discipline ('robot,' says Novak) that it's a wonder they still croak out their dismal hymns of a Sunday." *WASP*, as slang, connotes mannerisms of an uptight style of life.

WASP also revives another, but now bygone, figment of the sociological imagination—the supposedly homogeneous middle-class ways of life in suburbia, especially when contrasted to the working-class white ethnic "urban villages" of the central cities. In the 1950s, mainly urban intellectuals invented the "myth of suburbia" so they could hate it, and they clung to the myth in the face of all evidence. The suburban stereotype now has all the WASPs in affluence, working at bland corporation jobs, and rearing 2.0 children in isolated nuclear families. The culture critics' new anti-hero, the WASP, and the linking of WASPs to stereotypical suburban life styles represent a revival of the "myth of suburbia" and similarly serve ideological consistency.

WASPs, then, are uptight, arrogant, steady, compulsively hardworking, acquisitive automatons. Non-WASPs—the "real" ethnics—are effusive, impulsive, outgoing, warm, and kin-loving. The opposite of the WASP style conjures up the crude but popular Southern and Eastern European stereotypes. Sheed, in his review of the Schrag and Novak books, correctly observes that in trying to stereotype the WASP, the "real ethnics" are stereotyping themselves. The term *WASP* worked its way into trendy undergraduate textbooks for college courses all through the 1970s. We could guess that some old-fashioned ethnic stereotyping was just beneath the surface. And lo and behold, Novakism has raised its head in at least one textbook for undergraduates in social science. E. Barbara Phillips and Richard T. LeGates, in their *City Lights: An Introduction to Urban Studies* (1981), matter of factly speak of culture conflict "between the cool WASP and the emotional ethnic."

Social scientists have been explaining the perils of ethnic stereotypes for at least fifty years. Yet, as sociologist William Helmreich reminds us, stereotypes are both negative and positive and many have some basis in historical and ethnographic fact. The problem is that stereotypes, once they are allowed, invariably come to be used too simplistically and categorically and become pre-judgments about individuals or groups.

A few social scientists seem to have forgotten this lesson and are now saying that ethnic stereotypes are acceptable if they are positive. But deciphering what is a "positive" stereotype is a slippery business that invites immediate abuse. A "favorable" stereotype of "warm and emotional" easily slides into an unfavorable stereotype of "unstable and unreliable" and a stereotype of "cool" is but a short step from saying "unfeeling." Yet we are now urged to recognize supposed ethnic personality traits so as to facilitate better relations among groups and between individuals of different ethnic backgrounds. The ethnics are "emotional" and the WASPs are "cool," which supposedly helps to explain problems of interpersonal relations between individuals of these two groups. A few years ago it was faddish for astrology to be used in a similar way for instant understanding. Get their zodiac sign and that will tell you something about how you will get on with them and what to expect from them.

GUILTY *WASP*

In the early 1970s, when white Protestants spoke of themselves as *WASPs*, is was often in a context of expressing collective guilt for racism. Lois Mark Stalvey, who describes herself as a "German-American WASP" in her book *The Education of a WASP* (1970), says, "We are WASPs, my husband and I, lifelong members of the white Anglo-Saxon Protestant majority group, and some people say that it is primarily our group who created and continue 'white racism' in America." I have seen a few guilt-ridden intellectual whites of Protestant background turn the *WASP* invective on themselves in a genuine spirit of self-hatred, as though seeking atonement through self-flagellation.

I am also reminded of John Canaday's quaint confession of racial and ethnic naiveté in the *New York Times Magazine*, "A Wasp's Progress." The distinguished former art critic was perplexed that he was suddenly a member of an "unpopular minority group." "I am a Wasp, just the way other people who now outnumber me used to be niggers and kikes and wops and dagos." He felt put upon and said, "This is unfair, because although I am a Wasp, I am a nice Wasp." He documented this with childhood memories and anecdotes of his encounters with Catholics, Jews, and blacks in Fort Scott, Kansas, and pleaded that he was personally not guilty.

In 1977, Margaret Halsey published her stirring confession, *No Laughing Matter: The Autobiography of a WASP*, which includes a chapter titled "How to Raise a Prig." The ethnics message was definitely getting through to such thoughtful people. But most white Protestants absorbed the lesson at a different level, which gives the tale of *WASP* a final twist.

Ethnic epithets sometimes have the effect of a self-fulfilling prophecy. The targets began to think of themselves more consciously as the stereotype implied by the epithet. Ethnic epithets sometimes go through semantic inversion and the targets take the epithet as an ethnically proud self-descriptive and sometimes even mimic the caricature. I wonder how much the Preppy fad of the 1970s had to do with people playing the role of quintessential WASPs? At any rate, millions of white Protestants now cheerfully identify themselves as Wasps, proud of their honker ways, and the ethnics are vindicated in their original judgment.

NOTES

1. E. Digby Baltzell is sometimes credited with coining *WASP*, but he probably did not.

2. The *White* in *WASP* perhaps made more sense back in the early days when *WASP* was used only as an adjective, especially if one could think of it as having a series comma after the W— *W,ASP*.

AFTERWORD

This little book, especially the second half, has been a cautionary tale of how ethnic animosities can take many and devious guises in language. The old, crude ethnic slurs are not much heard these days, except as ugly taunts in the streets and, somehow more tragically, on college campuses in recent years. But a milder slang of ethnic abuse has entered academic jargon and popular discussions of social problems in the mass media. Ethnic biases in language are like sexist biases, using similar devices and artifices. People of good will are trying to free their speech and writing of sexist language. We can as well free our usage from implicit pejoration of ethnic groups.

APPENDIX

GOOD READING ON BAD WORDS

Ethnic slurs in American slang and other popular speech are treated in a variety of sources, all of which are readily available to the interested reader. H. L. Mencken was the first to give attention to homegrown terms of ethnic abuse in American English, beginning in the early editions of *The American Language*. The essays appear in their final form in the fourth edition and its two supplements. The abridged edition of *The American Language* (edited by the late Raven I. McDavid, Jr. in 1963), though, has most or all the material on terms of ethnic abuse.

Most ethnic slurs are collected in several dictionaries of American slang. The best is still Wentworth and Flexner's *Dictionary of American Slang* (second supplemented edition, 1975). Stuart Berg Flexner, the principal editor and compiler, enters 275 terms, and supplies authoritative dates of origin, etymologies, and examples of literary usages. Flexner also conveniently lists these words in the appendices, including an addendum in the supplement. Flexner's later book, *I Hear America Talking*, recounts a number of true stories about how ethnic slurs originated in the course of American social history.

In 1944 the psychologist Abraham A. Roback published

A Dictionary of International Slurs (reprinted in facsimile, 1979). Roback lists hundreds of ethnic slurs in their several forms and in a variety of modern languages, including American English. Richard A. Spear's dictionary of *Slang and Euphemism* (1981) lists about six hundred slurs in American English, which he collected from a variety of sources. The late Eric Partridge's monumental *A Dictionary of Slang and Unconventional English* (eighth edition, 1984), edited by Paul Beale, includes many American terms and is particularly useful for identifying ethnic epithets that we share with British, Canadian, and Australian English.

Many pejorative ethnic labels have American regional origins and associations, though many have also diffused in wider use. Frederic Cassidy's new four-volume *Dictionary of Regional American English* (volume 1, 1985; volume 2, 1990) is cumulating all such epithets. The new editions of the major unabridged dictionaries, such as *The Random House Dictionary of The English Language* (second edition, 1987), *The Oxford English Dictionary* (second edition, 1988), and *Webster's Third New International Dictionary* (1976), are all today more forthcoming in listing these offensive terms.

In good research libraries, the reader can find a backfile of *American Speech*, the official journal of the American Dialect Society, which now and then carries scholarly articles on ethnic labeling. *Maledicta*, which began publishing in 1977, is the only periodical that specializes in verbal aggression, including ethnic slurs, in all languages.

Finally, my book, *The Language of Ethnic Conflict* (1983), has a lexicon of more than one thousand ethnic epithets or names that have accumulated in historical American popular speech from the colonial period to about 1970. It also has a large bibliography on the language of ethnic abuse. Since its publication in 1983, I have found in addition perhaps a hundred less common epithets and a number of clarifying etymologies.

REFERENCES

Abrahams, Roger D. 1970. *Positively Black*. Englewood Cliffs, N. J.: Prentice-Hall.

———. 1980. "Folklore." In *Harvard Encyclopedia of American Ethnic Groups*, edited by S. Thernstrom et al., 370–79. Cambridge: Belknap Press of Harvard University Press.

———, and Susan Kalčik. 1978. "Folklore and Cultural Pluralism." In *Folklore in the Modern World*, edited by R. M. Dorson, 223–36. The Hague: Mouton.

Algeo, John. 1977. "Xenophobic Ethnica." *Maledicta* 1 (Winter):133–40.

Allen, Irving Lewis. 1983. *The Language of Ethnic Conflict: Social Organization and Lexical Culture*. New York: Columbia University Press.

Baker, Russell. 1978. "New York WASP." *New York Times* (July 18):A–17.

Baltzell, E. Digby. 1964. *The Protestant Establishment: Aristocracy and Caste in America*. New York: Random House.

Barnhart, Clarence L., Sol Steinmetz, and Robert K. Barnhart. 1973. *The Barnhart Dictionary of New English Since 1963*. New York: Barnhart/Harper & Row.

———. 1980. *The Second Barnhart Dictionary of New English*. New York: Barnhart/Harper & Row.

Bartlett, John Russell. 1877. *Dictionary of Americanisms: A Glos-

sary of Words and Phrases Usually Regarded as Peculiar to the United States, 4th ed. Boston: Little, Brown.

Bellow, Saul. 1964. *Herzog*. New York: Viking Press.

Berrey, Lester V., and Melvin Van Den Bark. 1953. *The American Thesaurus of Slang*. 2d ed. New York: Thomas Y. Crowell.

Berry, Brewton. 1963. *Almost White*. New York: Macmillan.

Bradley, Francis W. 1964. "Sandlappers and Clay Eaters." *North Carolina Folklore* 12 (December):27–28.

Brearley, H. C. 1973. "Ba–ad Nigger." In *Mother Wit from the Laughing Barrel*, edited by Alan Dundes, 578–85. Englewood Cliffs, N. J.: Prentice-Hall.

Campbell, John C. 1921. *The Southern Highlander and His Homeland*. New York: Russell Sage Foundation.

Canaday, John. 1972. "A Wasp's Progress." *New York Times Magazine* (March 19):32ff.

Cassidy, Frederic G. 1985–90. *Dictionary of American Regional English*. Vols. 1 and 2. Cambridge: Belknap Press of Harvard University Press.

Caudill, Harry M. 1963. *Night Comes to the Cumberlands: A Biography of a Depressed Area*. Boston: Little, Brown.

Ciardi, John. 1980. *A Browser's Dictionary*. New York: Harper & Row.

———. 1983. *A Second Browser's Dictionary*. New York: Harper & Row.

Claiborne, Robert. 1974. "A Wasp Stings Back." *Newsweek* (September 30):21.

Coles, Robert. 1971. *Migrants, Sharecroppers, Mountaineers*. Children of Crisis series, vol. 2. Boston: Little, Brown.

Colombo, John Robert. 1979. "Canadian Slurs, Ethnic and Others." *Maledicta* 3 (Winter):182–84.

Cooper, Joan. 1978. "A WECC (White English Celtic Catholic) Tells How It Is." *New York Times* (March 11):Op-Ed page.

Crowley, Ellen T., ed. 1982. *Acronyms, Initialisms, and Abbreviations Dictionary*. 8th ed. Detroit: Gale Research Company.

Dalby, David. 1972. "The African Element in American English." In *Rappin' and Stylin' Out*, edited by T. Kochman, 170–86. Urbana: University of Illinois Press.

Dickson, Paul. 1982. *Words*. New York: Delacorte Press.

Dillard, J. L. 1976. *Black Names*. The Hague: Mouton.

Dumas, Bethany K., and Jonathan Lighter. 1978. "Is *Slang* a Word for Linguists?" *American Speech* 53 (Spring):5–17.

Dundes, Alan. 1971. "A Study of Ethnic Slurs: The Jew and the Polack in the United States." *Journal of American Folklore* 84 (April–June):186–203.

Dundes, Alan, and Carl R. Pagter. 1975. *Urban Folklore from the Paperwork Empire*. Austin: American Folklore Society.

Dunlap, A. R., and C. A. Weslager. 1947. "Trends in the Naming of Tri-Racial and Mixed-Blood Groups in the Eastern United States." *American Speech* 22 (April):81–87.

Edwards, Owen. 1974. "The New York Wasp Is Not an Endangered Species." *New York* (August 12):27–32.

Eisiminger, Sterling. 1978. "Acronyms and Folk Etymology." *Journal of American Folklore* 91 (January–March):582–84.

Estabrook, Arthur H., and I. E. McDougle. 1926. *Mongrel Virginians: The Win Tribe*. Baltimore: Williams and Wilkins.

Flexner, Stuart Berg. 1975. "Preface." In *Dictionary of American Slang*, edited by H. W. Wentworth and S. B. Flexner, 2d supplemented ed., vi–xv. New York: Thomas Y. Crowell.

———. 1976. *I Hear America Talking*. New York: Touchstone/Simon and Schuster.

———. 1982. *Listening to America*. New York: Simon and Schuster.

Gerson, Louis L. 1964. *The Hyphenate in Recent American Politics and Diplomacy*. Lawrence: University of Kansas Press.

Halsey, Margaret. 1977. *No Laughing Matter: The Autobiography of a WASP*. New York: J. P. Lippincott.

Helmreich, William B. 1982. *The Things They Say Behind Your Back: Stereotypes and the Myths Behind Them*. New York: Doubleday & Co.

Higham, John. 1975. *Send These To Me*. New York: Atheneum.

Hoagland, Edward. 1988. " 'WASP' Stings. It Isn't Amusing." *New York Times*. (September 16):A–35. [Also see letter of response from Edith W. Kent, October 5, 1988, A–32].

Johnson, Diane. 1982. "Point of Departure" [a review of Saul Bellow's *The Dean's December*]. *New York Review* (March 4):6ff.

Johnson, Laurie. 1972. "Ethnic Awareness Praised as a Creative Force." *New York Times* (April 13):45.

Kephart, Horace. 1916. *Our Southern Highlanders*. New York: Outing Publishing Co. Reprint. Knoxville: University of Tennessee Press, 1976.

King, Florence. 1977. *WASP, Where Is Thy Sting?* New York: Stein & Day.

Lampe, Philip E. 1982. "Ethnic Labels: Naming or Name Calling?" *Ethnic and Racial Studies* 5 (October):542–48.

Larkin, Ralph W. 1979. *Suburban Youth in Cultural Crisis*. New York: Oxford University Press.

Leas, Susan E. 1981. "A Pronunciation of *Negro*." [Including Editor's Note by Charles Clay Doyle]. *American Speech*. 56 (Summer):154–55.

Lipski, John M. 1976. "Prejudice and Pronunciation." *American Speech* 51 (Spring–Summer):109–18.

McDavid, Jr., Raven I. 1960. "A Study in Ethnolinguistics." *Southern Speech Journal* 25 (Summer):247–54.

Mathews, Mitford M. 1975. "The Etymology of *Canuck*." *American Speech* 50 (Spring–Summer):158–60.

Mencken, H. L. 1963. *The American Language*, 4th ed., and the two supplements, abridged, with annotations and new material, by Raven I. McDavid, Jr., with the assistance of David W. Maurer. New York: Knopf.

Miller, Casey, and Kate Swift. 1977. *Words and Women*. Garden City, N. Y.: Doubleday/Anchor.

Mitford, Nancy, ed. 1955. *Noblesse Oblige*. Westport, Conn.: Greenwood Press.

Moody, Sid. 1983. "WASP: Are You Losing Thy Sting?" *Milwaukee Journal* (February 27): Life/Style, 1.

Morris, William, and Mary Morris. 1975. *Harper Dictionary of Contemporary Usage*. New York: Harper & Row.

———. 1977. *Morris Dictionary of Word and Phrase Origins*. New York: Harper & Row.

Newman, Edwin. 1977. *Strictly Speaking*. New York: Warner Books.

Novak, Michael. 1971. *The Rise of the Unmeltable Ethnics*. New York: Macmillan.

Opie, Peter. 1970. "Children's Derogatory Epithets." *Journal of American Folklore* 83 (July–September):345–55.

Orwell, George. 1946. "Politics and the English Language." In *The*

Orwell Reader, edited by Richard H. Rovere, 355–66. New York: Harcourt Brace Jovanovich, 1956.

Palmore, Erdman B. 1962. "Ethnophaulisms and Ethnocentrism." *American Journal of Sociology* 67 (January):442–45.

Partridge, Eric. 1984. *A Dictionary of Slang and Unconventional English*. 8th ed., edited by Paul Beale. New York: Macmillan.

Pederson, Lee A. 1964. "Terms of Abuse for Some Chicago Social Groups." *Publication of the American Dialect Society* 42 (November):26–48.

———. 1980. "Lexical Data from the Gulf States." *American Speech* 55 (Fall):195–203.

Phillips, E. Barbara, and Richard T. LeGates. 1981. *City Lights: An Introduction to Urban Studies*. New York: Oxford University Press.

Presley, Delma E. 1976. "The Crackers of Georgia." *Georgia Historical Quarterly* 60 (Summer):102–16.

Rawson, Hugh. 1981. *A Dictionary of Euphemisms & Other Doubletalk*. New York: Crown Publishers.

Redall, Henry Frederic. 1889. *Fact, Fancy, and Fable: A New Handbook for Ready Reference on Subjects Commonly Omitted from Cyclopaedias*. New York: A. C. McClurg & Co.

Roback, A. A. 1944. *A Dictionary of International Slurs*. Cambridge: Sci-Art Publishers. Reprint. Waukesha, Wisc.: Maledicta Press, 1979.

Robbins, Rossell Hope. 1949. "Social Awareness and Semantic Change." *American Speech* 24 (April):156–58.

Safire, William. 1980. "Breakdown in Morality." *New York Times* (March 6):A–23.

———. 1988. "1988's Results Today." *New York Times* (August 23):A–23.

———. 1989. "Parley in the Foothills." *New York Times Magazine* (October 15):16–17.

Schmemann, Serge. 1981. "Siberia a Refuge of Tramps, Traders and Tall Tales." *New York Times* (December 28):A–2.

Schrag, Peter. 1971. *The Decline of the WASP*. New York: Simon and Schuster.

Schuhmacher, W. W. 1989. "Once More *Canuck*." *American Speech* 64 (Summer):149.

Shapiro, Fred R. 1989. "Earlier Evidence for the Acronym WASP." *American Speech* 64 (Summer):189.

Sheed, Wilfred. 1972. "Wasp Wasting and Ethnic Upping." *New York Times Book Review* (June 4):2ff.

Simmen, Edward R. 1969. "*Chicano*: Origin and Meaning." *American Speech* 44 (Fall):225–27.

Spears, Richard A. 1981. *Slang and Euphemism*. Middle Village, N.Y.: Jonathan David Publishers.

Stalvey, Lois Mark. 1970. *The Education of a WASP*. New York: Bantam/William Morrow.

Strainchamps, Ethel. 1971. "Our Sexist Language." In *Woman in Sexist Society*, edited by V. Gornick and B. K. Moran, 240–50. New York: Basic Books.

Tarpley, Fred. 1970. *From Blinky to Blue-John: A Word Atlas of Northeast Texas*. Wolfe City, Tex: University Press.

Taylor, Sharon Henderson. 1974. "Terms for Low Intelligence." *American Speech* 49 (Fall–Winter):197–207.

Thernstrom, Stephan, Ann Orlov, and Oscar Handlin, eds. 1980. *Harvard Encyclopedia of American Ethnic Groups*. Cambridge: Belknap Press of Harvard University Press.

Todasco, Ruth, ed. 1973. *An Intelligent Woman's Guide to Dirty Words*. Vol. 1 of *The Feminist English Dictionary*. Chicago: Feminist English Dictionary.

Torres, Myriam. 1983. Private letter dated May 26, reporting data from the 1979 Chicano Survey conducted by the Institute of Social Research, University of Michigan, Ann Arbor, MI.

Totti, Xavier F. 1987. "The Making of a Latino Ethnic Identity." *Dissent* (Fall):537–42.

Trudeau, Pierre Elliott. 1977. A solicited letter to the editor under the heading, "Mr. Trudeau, What's a 'Canuck'?" *New York Times*, February 25, 23.

Watkins, Mel. 1971. "Finally the Wasp." *New York Times Book Review* (November 28).

Weed, Perry. 1973. *The White Ethnic Movement and Ethnic Politics*. New York: Praeger.

Wentworth, Harold, and Stuart Berg Flexner. 1975. *Dictionary of American Slang*, 2d supplemented ed. New York: Thomas Y. Crowell.

Wescott, Roger W. 1971. "Labio-Velarity and Derogation in English: A Study in Phonosemic Correlation." *American Speech* 46 (Spring–Summer):123–37.

Weseen, Maurice H. 1934. *A Dictionary of American Slang*. New York: Thomas Y. Crowell.

Wilmeth, Don B. 1981. *The Language of American Popular Entertainment*. Westport, Conn.: Greenwood Press.

Witchel, Alex. 1989. "Laughter, Tears and the Perfect Martini." *New York Times Magazine* (November 12):42ff.

INDEX OF SLUR-NAMES

AUTHOR-SUBJECT INDEX

About the Author

IRVING LEWIS ALLEN is professor of sociology at the University of Connecticut. He is the author of some forty articles, including "The Sociology of Slang" in the *Encyclopedia of Language and Linguistics*.